MW00603656

Miami Township
2718 Lyons Rd.
Miamisburg, Ohio 45342

Gems of the
Greater Dayton Region

Special Places Reflecting the Miami Valley's
Unique Natural and Cultural Identity

by Brian Hackett and Dane Mutter
Gail Horvath, Editor

First Edition
Allan L. Horvath Publications
Dayton Ohio

Bandshell at Island MetroPark (Murphy)

Gems of the Greater Dayton Region

Special Places Reflecting the Miami Valley's
Unique Natural and Cultural Identity

Acknowledgments
We would like to thank the following GEMS sponsors:

TURQUOISE
Craig Brown and Rebecca Appenzeller
DONet, Inc.
Downtown Dayton Partnership
Beth Grismer
Marlyn Jewelers
Bob Siebenthaler

AMETHYST
City of Dayton Commission
Dayton Area Chamber of Commerce
Gem Real Estate Group

TOPAZ
Aullwood Audubon Center and Farm
Five Rivers MetroParks
Tom Flynn
Kettering Health Network
Clay and MaryAnn Mathile
Benjamin Schuster
Jean Woodhull

SAPPHIRE
Beaver Creek Wetlands Association
Dayton Audubon Society
Julie C. Horvath
Larry Horvath

EMERALD
North American Nutrition Companies, Inc.

by Brian Hackett and Dane Mutter
Gail Horvath, Editor

Published by:
Allan L. Horvath Publications
137 N. Main Street Suite 206
Dayton, Ohio 45402, U.S.A.
email: ahp@germaine.net

Printed by: CJK Printing, Cincinnati, Ohio 45227, U.S.A.

Printed in the United States of America, First Edition 2007

ISBN-13: 978-0-9654152-2-4
Library of Congress Control Number: 2006938958

Foreword

Gems are treasures, jewels, valued possessions that can be admired, loved, prized and passed down to the next generation. The gems of the Greater Dayton Region beg to be explored, in print and in reality. These valued and diverse sites include natural wonders such as Cedar Bog, the Great Miami River and the Five Rivers MetroParks; museums like the Dayton Art Institute, the Dunbar House, the United States Museum of the Air Force and Boonshoft; and places of learning like our beloved Sinclair Community College.

Reading this book, our family remembered the regional bicentennial in 1996 when we chaired the celebration committee and learned about our founders who left behind Newcom Tavern. We recalled our family picnics to Germantown MetroPark, where we sought the trillium hillsides in early spring.

Leafing through the pages reminded us how we enjoy taking vicarious pleasure in the accomplishments of the Wright Brothers.

We appreciate, too, the people who have given leadership to boards and to programs that have developed and preserved our community treasures.

We urge readers to use this book as a guide. We want everyone to have enjoyable experiences such as ours.

David Ponitz, President Emeritus, Sinclair Community College
Doris Ponitz, community volunteer

Dayton was once aptly described as a gem of a city and it has remained the Gem City ever since. To those of us who have spent our entire lives here, it remains the brightest jewel in Ohio's crown.

David Greer

Dayton is indebted to E.J. (Joe) Koestner. During his 33 years as Director of the Dayton Museum of Natural History (now the Boonshoft Museum of Discovery), Koestner emphasized teaching nature, recruited enthusiastic volunteers and a remarkable staff, built the new museum and a planetarium, and moved the archives from the old library site to the new facility at Triangle Park.

Bill Hagenbuch

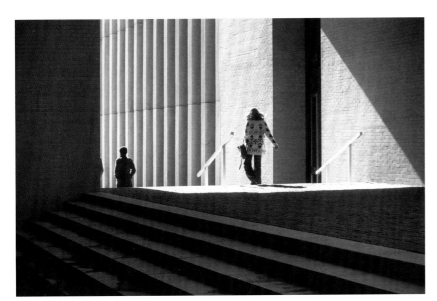

Downtown Dayton's Sinclair Community College, named for Scottish immigrant David A. Sinclair, and one of the largest community colleges in the U.S. (Horvath)

Whenever guests come from out of town, Carillon Park is a must-see attraction, with its free-standing exhibits ranging from the early pioneer era to the modern industrial revolution. Foreigners especially delight in seeing this glimpse of American history for themselves.

Manfred Orlow

Key Watershed References

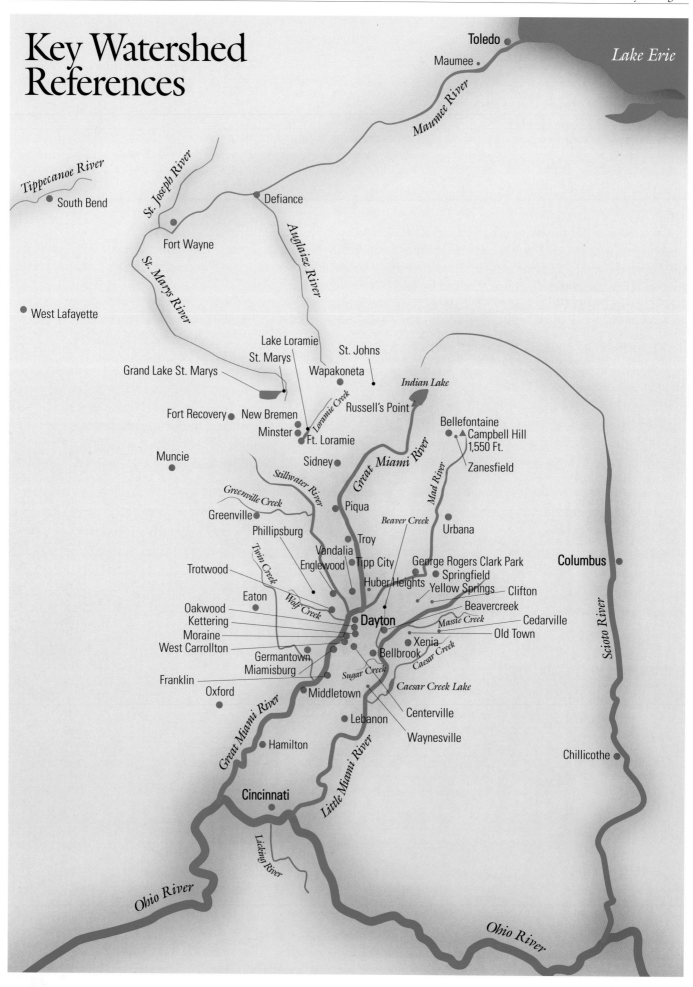

Lake Erie

Toledo

Maumee

Maumee River

Tippecanoe River

St. Joseph River

Defiance

South Bend

Anglaize River

Fort Wayne

St. Marys River

West Lafayette

Lake Loramie

St. Johns

St. Marys

Wapakoneta

Indian Lake

Grand Lake St. Marys

Russell's Point

Bellefontaine

▲ Campbell Hill
1,550 Ft.

Fort Recovery

New Bremen

Loramie Creek

Minster

Ft. Loramie

Zanesfield

Muncie

Sidney

Great Miami River

Mad River

Stillwater River

Greenville Creek

Piqua

Beaver Creek

Urbana

Greenville

Phillipsburg

Troy

Vandalia

Twin Creek

Englewood

Tipp City

George Rogers Clark Park

Columbus

Trotwood

Huber Heights

Springfield

Yellow Springs

Clifton

Eaton

Wolf Creek

Beavercreek

Oakwood

Dayton

Massie Creek

Cedarville

Kettering

Old Town

Scioto River

Moraine

Xenia

West Carrollton

Bellbrook

Germantown

Caesar Creek

Miamisburg

Sugar Creek

Franklin

Caesar Creek Lake

Centerville

Oxford

Middletown

Waynesville

Great Miami River

Lebanon

Hamilton

Little Miami River

Chillicothe

Cincinnati

Licking River

Ohio River

Ohio River

Brian Hackett

While Director of the Montgomery County Historical Society from 1992 to 2004, Brian Hackett was privy to the details and mysteries of one of the most beloved and significant gems of the region: the historic Old Courthouse. The offices, museum and collections of his organization were located there. What an experience, to come to work every day and walk up the steps of the place where Abraham Lincoln spoke to the crowds in 1859!

Dane Mutter

During his 21-year career with the Dayton-Montgomery County Park District, now Five Rivers MetroParks, Dane Mutter preferred to spend his time outdoors. Even as Assistant Director, he found reasons for escaping the office to explore the parklands. One of the area's natural gems he seems to be close to even today is the Stillwater River, which flows near his current home as well as near the MetroParks office. Though retired, he has not reformed his old ways. You have to catch him out on the trails somewhere!

Contents

John Bryan State Park (Horvath)

Old Montgomery County Courthouse, Dayton, corner of Third and Main, site of a courthouse since 1807 (Woody)

Introduction

On Coming Home

Whenever I get the chance to come to the Miami Valley, I always enjoy coming home.

I have always had a special feeling when I have come back to visit my family, friends and constituents, and those times have added richly to my life.

Every day that I have lived in Rome these past few years I've pulled up the *Dayton Daily News* online just to keep in touch. Although my job these past 28 years has forced me to live outside of the Miami Valley, it has also helped me to appreciate it better.

First, Greater Dayton is indeed a beautiful place, with the Miami and other rivers winding throughout the area, and its abundant parks dotting the landscape.

Second, we live in a place with a great history. Special people did wonderful things in the Miami Valley. People like Wilbur and Orville Wright, two very bright bicycle-maker brothers who decided to make an airplane that would fly, studied the problems involved and then actually did it. These brothers and their "Flying Machine" made air travel possible for the whole world.

It's the home of other inventors like Charles Kettering who got together a gang of friends and figured out how to avoid cranking the motor of an automobile by hand, thereby avoiding broken arms and making it possible for women to drive cars! Although less famous, Kettering and his gang changed the world, too.

Third, it's the place where "The Dayton Peace Accords" were brokered at Wright Patterson Air Force Base in 1995. After 250,000 people had died in the Balkans, just 21 days in Dayton put an end to that.

I would guess that local school children may know this history, and can rattle off some of the details like I did when I was a boy, but these things are truly world-changing events. My home town in the Miami Valley has quite a lot of which to be proud.

So when I come back for a weekend, I first always feel a great pride in my home region and what it has added to the world community.

Then, of course, so many of my favorite personal memories come to mind:

Memories of a wonderful childhood; of going to school in Kettering and the sports competitions with my brothers; and my folks cheering us from the stands during those great cool days of autumn. A great American childhood!

Dayton: Birthplace of Flight
(Mike Peters/courtesy of Dayton Daily News)

I am real proud of the Miami Valley and especially Downtown Dayton, where I've worked for 41 years in a 61-year-old family business.

Tim Pitstick

I love Downtown Dayton. It's been good to me and the building where I work is just great!

Ruth Bruns

I've known for years that the Dayton Club Building was formerly at First and Main, where the Barclay Building is now located. But I was surprised recently to learn that a stirring speech at the club on May 15, 1913 by Oakwood resident Adam Schantz, Jr. touched off the drive which led to the Miami Conservancy District.

Larry Suttman

In the 1940s, a three-cent trip on the streetcar took me into Downtown Dayton to the wonders of the era: the Biltmore and Van Cleve Hotels, Rike's, Keith's and Loew's Theaters, and the Arcade....Ah, those were the days!

John Lauferswiler

Downtown Dayton is in my blood. I wouldn't think of working anywhere else. Downtown is where everything happens.

Chuck Borgert

My wife and I like to go out to eat. Though we live in Yellow Springs, two of our favorite restaurants are in the Oregon District in Downtown Dayton: Jay's Restaurant and Pacchia.

Victor Garcia

My husband and I have been lifelong residents of the Dayton area and used to love taking our three sons to the Downtown Dayton Children's Parade the Sunday after Thanksgiving every year. Sometimes we'd have to take refuge inside Lazarus Dept. Store, where the Schuster Center is now located, because of inclement weather. Now our grandchildren attend the parade.

Ann Sortman

Coming back to Dayton never felt so good as after serving in the Peace Corps in Thailand, where life was so different from the America of the 1960s. It took me awhile to get readjusted to the everyday comforts we take for granted, and it was then that sparked the dawn of my public service. I will never forget the drive from Dayton up to the state legislature in Columbus; I can still do it with my eyes closed.

Sometimes when I come home, I drive by the house on St. Clair Street, where I was married to Janet Sue Dick, my wife of over 32 years. Dayton was where our daughter Jyl was born, and where so many friends came to cheer us during our son Matt's courageous battle with cancer.

I remember how excited we all were—but yet sad to leave Dayton—when we packed our things and moved to Washington in 1979, so I could serve as the U.S. Representative from Ohio's Third District. I never thought I would have been gone so long or that my career would take the turns that it did, but I'm grateful for all we got done, and what we have today as evidence of our work together.

Surely, seeing the Schuster Performing Arts Center and the Dayton Aviation Heritage National Historical Park is especially gratifying, given the Congressional work involved back when these important places were just ideas to visionary friends. These wonderful places give me great satisfaction as landmarks in our heritage, but my most treasured accomplishment from the Ohio Valley is the support that this community has given me in fighting for the world's hungry.

My passion changed when I went to Congress, and instead of giving me the boot, the community of Dayton encouraged me along the way to keep fighting for the poor, the widow, the orphan and those without hope. For 24 years Dayton kept sending me back to serve not just the Miami Valley, but the poor in the world. The people of Dayton provided a model example of a community that takes care of its own while reaching out to others.

Together we have made great progress in the fight against poverty, but there is still a long way to go. While we continue our work to end hunger in Ohio, in America and in the world, I will always look forward to the days ahead when I get to take a break from this labor and come home for a rest amongst my family, my friends and my community in Dayton. No matter where I live, the Miami Valley will always be home.

Tony P. Hall
Ambassador, United Nations, Rome, 2002-2006

Mead Theatre in the Benjamin and Marian Schuster Performing Arts Center, with theatre ceiling showing the stars at night as they appeared when the Wrights made their early flights (Wyckoff)

I have no doubt that the Schuster Center's Mead Theatre is the finest multi-purpose hall in the U.S. Moreover, when configured as a concert hall, I bet it's one of the top concert halls, too. The ceiling is lovely to look at, but it's also the key to the hall's acoustics, masking a massive chamber whose reverberation can be adjusted to suit the distinct sound needs of orchestra, opera and theater.

Neal Gittleman

A Dayton Metaphor. There once was a gem set in a ring of green countryside and farms. Later that ring became a beautiful silver setting for the gem. The ring itself got attention and the gem at the center began to lose its lustre. The gem was and remains the necessary center which provides national identity. If the gem is allowed to be damaged, the ring is inevitably tarnished.

[anonymous]

Stillwater River flood stage at Englewood MetroPark (Horvath)

Part One

Natural Gems of the Greater Dayton Region

Dane Mutter

Natural Diversity of the Area

When returning home to the Greater Dayton Region from other landscapes I have visited—Switzerland, Alaska, the Pacific Northwest, the U.S. Gulf Coast—I have always been impressed with the natural diversity of the Miami Valley, always. The Miami Valley is known for its rich soils, lush vegetation, rivers, streams and aquifers. What we lack in mountains and oceans we make up in mile after mile of beautiful, gently rolling, rural landscape and abundant wildlife. Birds! Over 270 species include summer visitors from South America, winter vistors from Canada and our own resident birds.

I see our natural gems as part of the established order of things. Some are complete systems, like our rivers and their watersheds that have changed very little over thousands of years. Others are merely remnants of large natural systems of pre-settlement days—old-growth forests, native prairies and wetlands.

Southwestern Ohio 450 Million Years Ago

We even have gems that lived millions of years in the past. Southwestern Ohio is well known for its abundance of well-preserved fossils, the remains of animals that lived here 425 to 450 million years ago.

Downy Woodpecker, common in Miami Valley (M. Welch)

While it was very nice to be in Europe, there is no place like home, right here in Dayton.

A.F. Foerste, who identified the rare trilobite fossil in 1919, on returning from trips to over 12 European countries around 1925

There are few places as nice as Englewood MetroPark, where I like to take long walks or bike rides.

Matt Irons

Ruby-crowned Kinglet, common migrant to the Miami Valley (M. Welch)

Huffman Dam at Huffman MetroPark, where 1919 trilobite was found (Makley)

Caesar Creek Trilobite, found in 1986, now at Boonshoft Museum of Discovery (De Young/courtesy of Dayton Society of Natural History)

My great-uncle, Cap Chambers, Chief Engineer for the Huffman Dam construction, was inspecting the project when he discovered the trilobite.

Charles Chambers

In the 1970s, my friends and I would camp out in Spooky Hollow in Waynesville, now known as the Caesar Creek Region. Camping at the top of the dark ravines, we listened to the flowing rivers and many night creatures. The screech owls would be screeching and our hearts would be pounding.

Jeffrey R. Huber

A large specimen of an unusual fossil was found in 1919 by workmen digging an outlet tunnel at the Huffman Dam construction site. Workmen brought the specimen to Arthur Morgan, Chief Engineer of all the dams. He then took it to August F. Foerste, an internationally famous geologist who was teaching at Steele High School in Downtown Dayton. Dr. Foerste identified the rare fossil, which finally landed in the Smithsonian Institute in Washington, D.C., where it remains one of the largest and most important trilobites of any kind ever found. Thanks to the efforts of teachers and students at Kettering's Beavertown School and Dayton's St. Anthony's School, the trilobite has been designated Ohio's State Fossil.

Fossil-hunting and Limestone

Fossil-hunting is a fantastic hobby. We are right in the middle of the famous solid limestone fossil beds that are visited by students and serious professionals from all over the globe, seeking these rare traces of early life. If we are curious about what is under the soil, we will find that anywhere we dig in the Miami Valley we will strike solid limestone bedrock, the natural foundation of Southwestern Ohio. The limestone was formed from sediments and the remains of sea animals that lived in one of the ancient oceans that occupied what we now call home. Fossil beds are best found where highways have cut through the horizontal rock layers or where streams have eroded away the soil. Many of the waterfalls in the Greater Dayton Region yield fossils. Some choice sites include the spillway at Caesar Creek State Park, Fossil Creek at Germantown MetroPark and many road cuts in the Dayton/Cincinnati region.

Southwestern Ohio, cephalopod and coral 450 million years ago (Mutter/courtesy of Carnegie Museum of Natural History)

Limestone is also the source of stone for roads and buildings like the Old Montgomery County Courthouse. The material for its construction was hauled, block by limestone block, by rail from a quarry in Centerville.

Caves

Caves are formed when rainwater travels through soil, absorbs carbon dioxide emitted from dead plants, comes to limestone and slowly creates an ever larger space as this slightly acidic water dissolves the limestone. The largest of the caves in Ohio are the Ohio Caverns, near West Liberty. The caves have a profusion of stalactite and stalagmite formations, and the air temperature is always 54 degrees F.

American Robin, harbinger of spring with its "cheer up, cheerio" song. (B. Welch)

Caesar Creek Reservoir, named after an African American who became a member of the Shawnee tribe (Baker)

Cedar Bog, a large freshwater fen near Urbana, dating from the last Ice Age (Mutter)

To build a log cabin, 40 or 50 trees must die. To build a Shawnee wickon, a dome-shaped house covered with bark, one large tree will die. Which way is more "primitive"? Which way, more "efficient"?

Chongo, Shawnee
United Remnant Band

Glaciers

Some 12,000 to 15,000 years ago, the massive Wisconsinan Glacier slowly melted and receded to the north, providing us with some of the best soils in the world and a great supply of gravel, sand and boulders. One of the finest examples of this is the huge glacial kame that begins at Calvary Cemetery in Dayton and extends southward to Rahn Road. This fine geologic "gem" of water-sorted sand, gravel and boulders was deposited by water flowing through ice tunnels in the once mile-high glacier. The top of the kame is some 200 feet above the present Miami River. The "Southern Hills" kame was once thought to be a moraine, and a city was even named after it. The hills to the east of the kame, starting south of Stewart Street, on Patterson Boulevard and extending to Franklin, Ohio are moraines. Moraines are the unsorted mix of stuff left by the glacier, something like the small pile of debris remaining in our yard after a large snowman melts.

Natural Springs

A close look at the region reveals sparkling natural springs. Natural springs usually occur at the base of ridges of glacial gravel, from which flows alkaline water rich in minerals.

The village of Yellow Springs gets its name from the natural spring nearby in Glen Helen. Big Spring, Montgomery County's largest spring, is located on Five Rivers MetroPark land near Aullwood Audubon Center and Farm.

Granite Boulders, ground smooth and transported by ancient glaciers, at Aullwood Farm (Mutter)

Gebhart Taven, built in 1811 in Miamisburg. Named for the Miami Indians nearby, Miamisburg was once called Hole's Station, after Zachariah Hole built a stockade and settled there around 1797. (De Young)

Clifton Gorge, a good example of limestone bedrock (Gross)

Cardinal, Ohio's State Bird, rare in early 1700s when Ohio was mostly forest. It likes edges of woodlands and back yards, and sings "birdy, birdy, birdy." (M.Welch)

My wife and I began going to Russell's Point, at Indian Lake, about 1950. There was an amusement park and a dance hall then. We became very fond of the lake and its surroundings.

Tony Furst

The Studebaker Wagon Company, starting from the 1850s, made horse-drawn wagons which were instrumental in making westward expansion possible. Many modern companies were founded by Studebakers, including Process Equipment Company and Spectra-Physics Laserplane (Trimble Navigation), both near Tipp City. The Studebaker National Museum in South Bend, Indiana tells the story from wagons to cars. Hundreds of Studebaker descendants live in Miami County and in Indiana.

Miriam Owen Irwin

Early Settlers

Early settlers heading west discovered a great expanse of rich, deep soil in the natural region of Ohio now called the Glacial Till Plains. After they rode over the Appalachian foothills in creaking covered wagons, or poled a pirogue up the Great Miami or Scioto River, the first settlers encountered mostly dense forest, and a few wetlands and prairies. The forests were filled with bear, deer and other game. There were also buffalo and elk, ducks and geese. Pioneers had to watch out too for wolves, wildcats, rattlesnakes and unfriendly Indians.

Virgin Hardwoods vs. Farms

Most pioneers dreamed of a place of their own in this new world paradise. Backbone, grit and a sharp axe were prime requirements to make way for a farm, with maybe a few acres of corn, some vegetables and a small field of grass for horses and other livestock. Huge trees were downed. Some were needed for a cabin and shelter for horses and some livestock. The rest were simply in the way. Massive log piles were burned. Destruction of the virgin hardwoods took a little over 50 years.

Principal Watersheds

A watershed is any stream or river with all of the land that drains into it. Our Miami Valley generally includes the Great Miami River and the Little Miami River watersheds, which cover some 7,140 square miles of Southwestern Ohio.

Indian Lake, Where the Great Miami River Begins

Indian Lake is the headwater source of the Great Miami River. Indian tribes lived and hunted there. The Old Indian Lake (one of five small natural lakes there), being close to the Miami River, was part of the Indian trade route between the Ohio River and Lake Erie. In 1851 work began, to make it one of the many reservoirs that supplied water for the famous Miami-Erie Canal. The reservoir was also called Lewistown Reservoir, named for Shawnee leader Captain John Lewis, whose village of Lewistown is nearby. Indian Lake Dam creates the modern Indian Lake: a resort area, fishing spot and an Ohio State Park.

Eldean Bridge, Ohio's second longest covered bridge, over Miami River near Troy (Wyckoff)

Great Miami River near Troy (Wyckoff)

Winter on the Stillwater River (Horvath)

Great Miami River

Blackhawk Run, Van Horn Creek and the North and South Forks of the Great Miami River are headwater streams that flow into Indian Lake. The channel that flows out is where the Miami begins its 170.3-mile journey to the Ohio River. Cherokee Man's Run is the first tributary flowing into the Great Miami, just over 100 yards below the "bulkhead" (dam). More tributary streams with names like Blue Jacket Creek, Flat Branch and McKees Creek join the River, as they trickle and flow down the west slope of Campbell Hill a few miles southeast of Indian Lake. Fishermen say the Great Miami has a greater variety of fish than the entire state of Colorado and offers some of the best smallmouth bass fishing in Ohio.

Mad River

Campbell Hill is Ohio's highest point (1,550 feet above sea level). The raindrops that roll down the east side become the Mad River. This is the same Mad River that flows into the Great Miami. Cool groundwater flows into the Mad River from the deep glacial deposits and this brings great pleasure to trout fishermen. Experts say the Mad is one of the few Ohio streams capable of supporting a naturally reproducing population of brook trout. It is also a "gem" of a stream for canoeing. Geologists believe that several thousand years ago the Mad was much larger than the Great Miami. They estimate its flow at more than 100 times what it is today.

Stillwater River

The adventuresome will take their kayaks or canoes up to Darke and Northwestern Miami County. An exciting downstream float trip would be on Greenville Creek or its parent stream, the Stillwater River. Both of these gems are designated Ohio Scenic Rivers. En route one can enjoy the Miami County Park District's Greenville Falls near Covington. The Stillwater River and the Mad Rivers join the Great Miami in Downtown Dayton.

Geese at Spring Lake Park, Bellbrook (Caffrey)

When I was in high school in 1947, I purchased a used Old Town canoe from the Dayton Canoe Club, fixed it up and renamed it Tondeleo. I enjoyed canoeing upstream on the Stillwater River from Island Park where I stored the canoe in a boat locker, but I cannot remember ever being able to get past the rapids in the shallow section by the Siebenthaler Bridge.

Roy Horvath

Great Miami River and Dayton skyline from the Dayton Art Institute (Ponikwia)

My father, who was in the Navy in Chicago, was sent to Dayton with other men in 1913 to help out after the flood.

Phyllis DePear Horvath

Trailsend, former home of Gov. James M. Cox, on Governor's Trail in Kettering (Woody)

Democrat James M. Cox is known as a progressive three-term Ohio Governor, a former schoolteacher and candidate for President, who started what is now the Dayton Daily News in 1898, and was involved in creating the Miami Conservancy District and the City of Dayton Airport.

Ben Kline

Price Brothers moved to Dayton after the flood, looking for construction opportunities. They found one: supplying and installing precast concrete blocks, threaded on steel cables, to provide flexible mats that protect the beaches and levees from erosion. This innovative project was the start of a long and successful relationship with Dayton.

Gayle Price, Jr.

The Great 1913 Flood

In March 1913 heavy rain on frozen ground caused the waters of the Miami, Stillwater and Mad Rivers to flood Dayton and other cities in the Miami Valley. Some 478 lives were lost, and damage exceeded $100,000,000. It was the worst disaster ever to hit the Greater Dayton Region. That tragedy, however, led to the creation of our wonderful system of parks.

Five Dams Constructed

The 1913 crisis stimulated men like John Patterson, Adam Schantz, Colonel Edward Deeds, Governor James Cox and Arthur Morgan to take action. The Miami Conservancy District was formed as the first watershed district in Ohio. Arthur Morgan became the first Chief Engineer. Land was purchased for construction of five world-class flood control dams: Englewood, Taylorsville, Huffman, Germantown and Lockington. These dams have saved the Miami Valley untold millions of dollars in flood losses since 1913.

Setting Aside Land for Recreation

I visited the late Arthur Morgan at his home in Yellow Springs when he was 96. He told me of his decision to save the lands bordering the flood control dams for future recreation use. He said, "I stood firm against the wishes of my Board at the risk of being fired, because I believed in the future of recreation land in the Miami Valley. That's why you have good parks today."

In the early days of the Dayton-Montgomery County Park District, now Five Rivers MetroParks, we often used the phrase "instant parks." I was with the Park District 21 years, starting in 1967. That year we signed a long-term lease with the Miami Conservancy District, creating 2,532 acres of instant parks for people to enjoy hiking, fishing, picnicking, dog-walking, nature at its best on the same acres that Dr. Morgan set aside years ago.

Deeds Carillon at Carillon Park (Wyckoff)

Martindale Falls at Englewood MetroPark (Murphy)

Three Sisters, white oaks at Sugarcreek MetroPark (Brewer)

Osage-orange tunnel at Sugarcreek MetroPark (Caffrey)

Outstanding Gems

In the Greater Dayton Region, we have outstanding examples of old-growth forests, native prairies and wetlands. For many, a short drive or bike ride will take us from an urban or suburban home to an amazing place reminiscent of the Miami Valley in the late 1700s, before the white settlers arrived on the scene.

Forests

Accounts written by early settlers tell of their awe at the giant trees—beech, maple, hickory, oak, tulip, ash, walnut, wild black cherry and more. Many trees were 150 feet tall and a few even taller. History tells of giant chestnut trees, long since killed off by a European blight. The native hardwood forest where the newcomers began to cut openings for cabins and farms surpassed all others in the world for variety and size of trees.

Germantown MetroPark

One old-growth forest is in Germantown MetroPark, near Germantown Dam. The term "old-growth" means just that: large old trees that have matured since the virgin timber was cut early in the 19th century.

The forest is fascinating any time of year. In April to early May, before the leaves on the trees form, spring beauties, trillium, bloodroot, twin-leaf, Dutchman's breeches and many other early wildflowers appear. By the time the forest is fully leafed and has become dark and cool, the migrating birds have all returned and have built their nests. Forest nesting birds are hard to locate but be assured they are there. Serious birders have found at least 146 species in the Germantown woods. Fall color is spectacular and winter is the perfect time for a brisk hike in the woods.

Twin Creek, the second most biologically diverse stream in Ohio, flows through the forest at Germantown.

Luna Moth. Nocturnal, it likes hardwood forests. Its adult life span is only one week, during which it must find a mate. (B. Welch)

We have many fond memories of the Sugarcreek Reserve, traipsing with our young children through the woods, wading in the creek, observing the wild creatures. One of our children's favorites was the Three Sisters, the giant ancient oak trees which have become a landmark in the reserve. To a small child (or an adult), these huge majestic trees certainly make a lasting impression.

Pete and Paula DiSalvo

Germantown MetroPark is the most diverse and important natural area managed by the MetroParks.

Dave Nolin

Germantown MetroPark (Horvath)

Sunfish Pond at Germantown MetroPark (Brewer)

Prairie at Aullwood Audubon Center and Farm, with Marie Aull and Paul E. Knoop, Jr. (photographer unknown)

Marie Aull's dream was to have this special place for children to come and experience nature. That's what it's all about for me.

Tom Hissong

Aullwood Audubon Center and Farm's hands-on programs have been inspiring, teaching and involving youngsters and adults for the last three generations, spanning 50 years and changing lives to make positive conservation actions for the earth.

Charity Krueger

After the virgin timber was cut in the early to mid-19th century, white-tailed deer, pileated woodpeckers and beaver were completely gone from the Valley, only to return in large numbers when their habitat was restored. Wild turkey, short-eared owls, possum, raccoon, gray squirrels and many other forest-dwelling animals also live here.

I remember seeing two coyotes chasing a deer in the snow in a Germantown meadow. The deer eventually escaped, though in the natural scheme of things coyotes are needed to control the herds.

Prairies

The same pioneers that were awed by our virgin forests were baffled by the large open areas with no trees. Most assumed that if the soil were too poor to grow trees, it would be too poor to farm. The opposite is true. Soil scientists find prairie soils to be some of the most fertile land on the planet.

Spring is not the best time to see a prairie. As winter fades in the treeless prairie, a brown background of dry grasses and herbs emerges, but there is promise. The mix of beautiful green prairie plants always returns and in midsummer, to our delight, the blooms attract a variety of butterflies.

The Prairie at Aullwood Audubon Center and Farm

The first restored prairie in Ohio is located at Aullwood Audubon Center and Farm. In the 1960s Paul E. Knoop, Jr., then educational director at Aullwood, planted the prairie on an old crop field on the former John Aull farm. It took several years to establish but the results rewarded the hard work—prairie grasses taller than a man on horseback, a rainbow of color in a variety of flowering plants carefully chosen to represent a native Ohio prairie.

Next door to Aullwood Audubon Center and Farm is Aullwood Garden MetroPark, where the former home of John Aull watches over the garden that he and his wife Marie developed together. In 1922 John was the owner of Aull Brothers Paper Box Company. He drove to Cincinnati regularly to court Marie Sturwold after they met on an exciting trip to Alaska. Marie and John were married in June 1923. John and Marie Aull found they had a common passion: gardening. They set about developing the woodland garden below their home, and from the start opened it to the public.

Marie was a hands-on gardener and often gave talks and demonstrations about gardening to the Garden Club of Dayton, to other clubs, and informally at her own garden.

Former home of John and Marie Aull, Aullwood Garden MetroPark (Horvath)

When I enter the grounds of Aullwood Garden, a sense of calm washes over me. I take a deep breath and instinctively know the connection to nature Marie must have felt tending to her garden.

Mary Klunk

I've visited a lot of gardens around the world, but Mrs. Aull's garden is a world-class garden in every respect.

Bob Siebenthaler

Marie's spirit pervades all that is at Aullwood, from the hellebores breaking through the snow, to the magnificent sycamore which symbolizes her life.

Julia Hobart

EDITOR'S NOTES:

The Garden Club of Dayton was founded in June, 1922 by Katherine Houk Talbott, the wife of engineer Harold E. Talbott, Sr. The Talbotts' home, Runnymede, located on a hill in Oakwood, was a safe haven for people fleeing the floodwaters. In the 1940s the Runnymede Playhouse (a separate auditorium building on the Talbotts' property), was the site of polonium research in connection with the Manhattan Project.

The Talbotts and the Aulls were friends. Katherine Talbott encouraged Marie Aull to join the Garden Club of Dayton, shortly after Marie's marriage in 1923. Marie became a life-long member. John Aull's first marriage was to Mary Harries, whose father Frank built the Harries Building (the current Barclay Building) in Downtown Dayton in 1925. Coincidentally, this editor's office is located in the Barclay Building, and is a block away from Talbott Tower, named after the Talbott family.

Carlton W. Smith, who donated Smith Memorial Gardens to the City of Oakwood in 1975, said it best when he described the gardens, at the corner of Oakwood Avenue and Walnut Lane, as "an intimate setting and strolling place of rest...an open, green, colorful, quiet retreat on a busy street...a breathing space of green shade and color for busy people."

Carol Collins

Huffman Prairie Flying Field and replica of Wright Brothers' Hangar at Wright-Patterson Air Force Base, interpretive center not shown (Nolin)

Huffman Prairie is sacred ground for those who cherish the dream of flight.

It was here, in 1904 and 1905, that the Wright Brothers transformed the marginal success achieved at Kitty Hawk, North Carolina in 1903 into the reality of a practical airplane. In the air over this Ohio cow pasture, an airplane made the first flight lasting over a minute, flew the first full circle, and first remained aloft for an hour.

How appropriate that this historic spot is surrounded by modern Wright-Patterson Air Force Base, a facility dedicated to the achievement of the technology that was born here!

Tom Crouch

Rediscovery of Huffman Prairie and Beaver Creek Wetlands

Two additional natural gems are must-see places. The first is Huffman Prairie, the largest native prairie in Ohio and the site of the Wright Brothers' flying field. The second is the Beaver Creek Wetlands.

The reason these prairie and wetland gems are thriving natural areas today, and not a hayfield or a golf course, is credited to David Nolin. As a Wright State University graduate student in the 1980s, he was curious about the location of natural systems before the arrival of our early pioneers. With the help of his advisor, Dr. James Runkle, he interpreted the 1802 records of Israel Ludlow, a surveyor and credible naturalist who outlined prairie and wetland borders on his primitive maps.

From Ludlow's early notes Nolin made a map showing the old locations of prairies and wetlands in the Mad River Valley and some of the Little Miami River Valley as well. After a year searching these sites for prairie and wetland remnants, he rediscovered Huffman Prairie and the Beaver Creek Wetlands.

Huffman Prairie Flying Field

By the 1980s the wet prairie flying field had become part of the massive Wright-Patterson Air Force Base. It had been drained, runways were constructed and the actual site of the Wrights' flying field and Huffman Prairie had become a hayfield. By mere chance Nolin visited the old flying field when the mowing crew was apparently behind schedule and he was able to view about 100 acres of tall grass prairie precisely on the site of Ludlow's old 1802 map. After some discussion, Wright-Patterson Air Force Base administrators accepted the idea of establishing a native prairie on the base. In 1986 Huffman Prairie became a State Natural Landmark.

Little Miami River

Beaver Creek, where the Beaver Creek Wetlands are located, is a tributary of the Little Miami River. Beaver Creek joins the Little Miami River near the city of Beavercreek.

Rivers can be young, middle-aged and old, all at the same time. At its youngest stage, the Little Miami River flows from springs in the hills east of Springfield and near South Charleston in Eastern Clark County. It is said that the second wife of frontiersman Simon Kenton saw these spring fields 200 years ago and named the settlement there "Springfield." The spring fields give rise to a 105-mile stretch of the river.

Huffman Prairie (Nolin)

Black Swallow-tail butterfly on prairie coneflower at Huffman Prairie (Nolin)

There is a place in Clifton Gorge where it is said a white man fleeing from Shawnee Indians jumped across the gorge, narrowly making it, but escaping to Kentucky and freedom.

Harry O'Roark

Fifteen miles downstream, the river behaves like a giddy teen-ager, a veritable mountain stream as it swirls and plunges through Clifton Gorge. A short distance below Glen Helen, near Yellow Springs, the river becomes middle-aged. It gains volume from Massie Creek and Beaver Creek, rushes through the "narrows" near Indian Ripple Road and flows on through riffles and pools, meandering over gently rolling farmland on its way to the Ohio River. In the lower reaches, the Little Miami has some long pools with little current. It is very close to the same elevation of the parent Ohio River and that's a sure sign that the energetic, middle-aged scenic river has now reached senior status.

The Great Miami and the Little Miami Rivers provide parallel, almost identical, natural watercourses to carry the excess rainfall of Southwestern Ohio into the Ohio River.

Sport fishermen are fond of the Little Miami. Some of the best canoeing and kayaking in Southwestern Ohio begin at local liveries on the middle stretches of the river. Little Miami Incorporated, one of the oldest river preservation groups in Ohio, has done extraordinary work in preserving the wooded lands adjacent to the river. Much of the corridor has been acquired by purchase or conservation easement for future protection of this beautiful stream.

Fishing on the Little Miami River (Horvath)

Birch Creek at Glen Helen (Draeger)

Fairborn Marsh, Beaver Creek Wetlands (Swigart)

Damsel Fly at Beaver Creek Wetlands (Swigart)

Beaver Creek Wetlands

Late August and September are great times for a visit to the wetlands. The Beaver Creek Wetlands in Greene County offers a comfortable, accessible boardwalk for the best view of a fresh water fen in our immediate area. Here the late summer wildflowers of the wetlands grow in a habitat like no other—in wet, cool, saturated soil, and shallow standing water.

Most of the wetland is intimately linked to the groundwater which comes to the surface from a great underground source called an aquifer. This aquifer is also the source of drinking water for much of the region. The aquifer is recharged when there is excess rainfall. Wetlands help protect this source. Some of the rarest communities of plants and animals are found where gently flowing alkaline groundwater rises to the surface over a large area. These areas are called fens.

Watch for changes in habitat. Swamps—wooded areas with standing water—are great places for wood ducks, woodpeckers and salamanders. Trees like cottonwood, green ash, silver maple and box elder are found here.

Marshes with their reedy vegetation—cattails, sweet flag and burr reed—are good places to find wading birds and amphibians.

Sedge meadows—sites dominated by low, grass-like sedges—have a profusion of flowering plants from mid- to late summer.

Shrub-scrub zones—where dense shrubby cover protects many birds that nest or rest in the wetlands—display the pink bloom of swamp rose, queen of the prairie, and the bright yellow flowers of shrubby cinquefoil.

Great Blue Heron at Beaver Creek Wetlands (Swigart)

Beaver Creek Wetlands (Amon)

Cox Arboretum and Garden MetroPark is a leading landscape arboretum, connecting people with nature, teaching respect for the land, and demonstrating sustainable horticulture.

Jay Woodhull

The traditional Indian way of farming was to plant in clusters, with three to six feet in between. In each cluster, we planted some corn in the center. When the stalks were knee-high, we planted beans. When the beans sprouted and climbed the stalks, we planted squash and pumpkins around the outside to stop the weeds. Dried fish was used as a fertilizer rather than manure, to avoid introducing other plants or weeds.

Dark Rain Tom

Modern Farming

Today agriculture in the Greater Dayton Region is flourishing. From an era of agricultural dominance from the mid-1850s up to World War I, the land use trend has gone slowly to fewer and larger farms. In the 1930s and 1940s a general farmer could make a living on less than 100 acres. Now 1,500 to 2,000 acres are needed. The reduction of farm acres has prompted incentive programs to rural landowners to sell agricultural easements to the United States Department of Agriculture. Farmers retain ownership but may only use the land for agricultural purposes. This is significant, and prompted by the need to produce food for an ever-growing world population.

Trends

Where our forefathers and mothers cut trees to live, current residents now plant trees in large numbers to create a pleasant aesthetic. Today one of the most lucrative agricultural enterprises in this area is the production, sale and planting of nursery and landscape plants. Other agricultural trends show a marked increase in the production of corn and soybeans, while livestock farms have decreased dramatically.

Cox Arboretum MetroPark (Worman)

Fulton Farms (Wyckoff)

When I worked at Possum Creek MetroPark, it was fun to hear the kids cry out to their friends things like "Do you see how big that cow is?" and "That's a pig?"

Ann Horvath

Every day near Lebanon I pass some fruit farms where people are often picking strawberries or buying fresh produce.

Mujgan Inciler

One of my favorite memories of our childhood home on Belmonte Park North near the Art Institute involves the three crabapple trees in the back yard. In the spring, their blossoms were beautiful. In late summer, the trees were filled with fruit which Mother transformed after many hours in a hot, sticky kitchen into smooth, delicious jelly.

Mary Gnau Richard

John Chapman, called "Johnny Appleseed" because of his 50 years of planting apple trees in the Northwest Territory, celebrated annually by the Johnny Appleseed Festival in Fort Wayne, Indiana, where he died (L. Ostendorf)

Urbana University chose to open the Johnny Appleseed Museum here because of its close ties with Johnny. Johnny was a missionary for the Swedenborgian Church that founded the University in 1850 and he distributed its religious material throughout the Ohio Territory during his lifetime (1774-1845). He was good friends with the university's founder, Col. John James, and with its first president, Milo Williams, whom he had met through his family and through the church.

Joe Besecker

Riverscape, Downtown Dayton, invention station for the self-starter in background (Wyckoff)

Unique Farms

Several unique farms invite visitors, especially school classes and families, to see first-hand the important link between our food, rich soil and water resources. Aullwood Audubon Center and Farm near Englewood has a working organic farm complete with farm animals and a working "sugar bush" for the production of maple syrup. Carriage Hill Farm, a Five Rivers MetroPark facility located in Huber Heights, is a working farm of the 1880s, with year-round demonstrations ranging from sheep-shearing in the spring to making sausage and lard in the fall. Much of the field work is done with draft horses. MetroPark's Possum Creek Farm in Jefferson Township appeals to families with children. It has a wide variety of farm animals and presents opportunities for getting up close. A modern dairy may be seen near Yellow Springs at Young's Jersey Dairy.

The Dull Farm Homestead

The Dull Homestead, located a few miles west of Englewood on the Old National Trail highway, yields an unusual harvest. Six 120-foot-high wind turbines produce about 57,000 kilowatts (KW) of electricity per year. (My home uses 14,800 KW per year.) This is the home of the Future Energy Center. The center office and the Dull Farm office use the fuel and hot water generated from a stationary hydrogen unit. The unit is fueled by electricity with wind and solar energy providing power at optimum times.

Urban Natural Spaces

Our cities have bike trails, hiking trails, riverscapes and parklands for residents to enjoy. Wildlife viewing does not stop at the city limits. Loft dwellers in Dayton may view ospreys diving into the Great Miami River for a meal, and then may sight a peregrine falcon—fastest bird in the world—swooping at 200 mph to catch a pigeon on the wing in the shadow of the Kettering Tower.

Learning Tree Farm's mission is to facilitate hands-on learning experiences in a traditional farm setting.

Sally Keyes

For 30 years my family has sought the peace of a natural setting in Grant Park—an oasis nestled in the heart of Centerville/ Washington Township.

Betty Snyder

At least one weekend a year, my friends and I bike the Community Trail from Springfield to Cincinnati. There are great places to stop and eat and the scenery is beautiful, especially along the Great Miami River.

Stephen A. Penny

Great Miami River Corridor Classic (Horvath)

Riverscape, and Great Miami River (curving northward); Deeds Point, Mad River (curving eastward) (Makley)

I'm not surprised that Indian tribes reserved the lands between the Miamis for hunting. It was not unheard of. Indeed what is now the largest part of Kentucky was once a sacred hunting ground for all Indians, but with no permanent villages. That's why it was so attractive to early settlers like Daniel Boone, and why the Indians would raid the settlements on the Kentucky frontier from their villages in Ohio.

Brian Hackett

John Bryan State Park is our favorite place to camp and go for a hike.

Rose Chable

State and Regional Parks

Thousands of acres of large state and regional parks await our visit anytime. Every park is unique. Sycamore State Park, for example, on Diamond Mill Road in Trotwood, was dedicated in 1979 and contains over 2,300 acres of land, including Green Meadows, the former Girl Scout Farm property and barn from the 1950s. It borders 3.5 miles of Wolf Creek and has trails for hikers and horseback riders, and opportunities for fishing, hunting, camping, sledding, skiing and ice-skating.

Native Americans Valued Region

Long ago Native Americans recognized the special nature of this region. Historians say that from the 1700s until the arrival of the white settlers, no villages were established by area tribes, by some kind of unspoken agreement, in the lands between the two Miami Rivers. These lands, from the Ohio River north to the Mad River, were mostly dense forest filled with game, but the Indians hunted only what they needed and then moved on, leaving the abundant wildlife for others to share.

Sailing on Acton Lake at Hueston Woods State Park (Horvath)

Understanding Our Connection

Native Americans understood their connection to the natural world around them. The Amish, too, have a spiritual relationship with the earth and it is reflected in their simple lifestyle. This understanding is echoed by modern-day environmentalists and outdoor educators at centers like the Aullwood Audubon Center and Farm in Dayton, the Brukner Nature Center in Troy and the Glen Helen Outdoor Education Center in Yellow Springs.

During a seminar at Bergamo Center and Carriage Hill MetroPark a few years ago, Father Thomas Berry summed up his philosophy on environmental consciousness with the following words. "The natural world is the larger sacred community to which we belong. To be alienated from this community is to become destitute in all that makes us human. To damage this community is to diminish our own existence." (Thomas Berry, *The Dream of the Earth*).

Unique Riches

I am always impressed with the natural diversity of this region: its beautiful rolling hills, lush vegetation, streams and abundant wildlife. Residents of the Miami Valley today are indeed blessed by the region's richness and natural diversity. In my opinion, it rivals that of any other region in the U.S.

In my mind, the wonderful and precious natural lands that encircle our city—the mighty convergent rivers, the parks and green spaces—are special because they lend meaning to all of our lives.

Paul E. Knoop, Jr.

Hiking in the Five Rivers MetroParks is like going on a Volksmarsch in Germany.

Ten-year-old Kyle Grosselin

Children's Discovery Garden at Wegerzyn Gardens MetroPark (J. Ostendorf/ Wegerzyn Gardens)

There were two main types of canal boats: those to transport passengers and those to transport freight. The boats were 14 feet wide. Each boat had a tow rope which was connected to horses or mules who were driven or ridden by a driver along a ten-foot-wide towpath on one side of the canal. The water in the canal was about four feet deep and came from feeder channels connecting the nearby rivers to the canals. Most work constructing the canals was done by hand, by newly arrived immigrants from Ireland, Germany and France, and by local farm boys. The speed of travel was about three miles an hour. Toll collectors would collect fees from passing canal boats. (John H. Patterson was a toll collector early in his career.)

Over 100 locks at different intervals raised the water level. At its highest point, at Loramie Summit, it was 512 feet above the Ohio River. The gradual climb to the summit by the canal represented an elevation equivalent to a 50-story building. In order to cross rivers, 19 aqueducts were built: wooden troughs constructed over the rivers. Alongside each aqueduct's waterway was a wooden path for the

Miami-Erie Canal at Piqua's John Johnston Farm, home of Ohio's only Indian agent, who is said to be one of the few whites that Indians respected. Johnston's daughter Julia married Jefferson Patterson, the son of Col. Robert Patterson. Julia and Jefferson became the parents of John H. Patterson of NCR. (Wyckoff)

Canal boat captains did not have it easy. Whenever they came to a lock, they only had six inches on each side for clearance, since the locks were only 15 feet wide. In addition, when one boat met another going in the opposite direction, the crew might have to fight the other boat's crew, literally, for right of way. Theoretically, the boat going downstream was to let its tow rope sink to the bottom of the canal, to let the other boat pass. But the process took time and time was valuable even then.

Dave Neuhardt

horse and driver to use as they towed the canal boat. One aqueduct carried the canal over the Mad River in Downtown Dayton where Rita Street (if it extended beyond Valley Street) would cross over. Once south of the Mad River, the canal turned west and an extension passed alongside Barney & Smith Car Works, where the City of Dayton's maintenance yard is now located, near Ottowa Street and east of the Keowee and Monument Ave. corner.

Three reservoirs provided water to the Miami-Erie Canal during times of low water - at Indian Lake, and St. Marys and Loramie reservoirs. Canals were more convenient than traditional river transportation because of the growing number of dams built on rivers to harness water for mills. In the winter, the canals would freeze up and provide opportunities for skating and sleigh-riding. In the summer, the water was great for wading and swimming, even, it is said, in the aqueducts, across the Mad River, the Miami River or Loramie Creek.

Battle of Peckuwe re-enactment at George Rogers Clark Historic Park (Lackey/courtesy of Springfield Sun News)

Miamisburg Mound, largest conical Indian burial mound in Ohio (De Young)

Part Two

Cultural and Historical Treasures

Brian Hackett, with Gail Horvath

Old Chillicothe

Near the city of Xenia, there is a very old and special place. To the Shawnee who once walked, hunted and farmed this land, the name they gave it meant "principal fire" or "principal gathering place." The Americans who came to settle this same ground in the 1700s would incorrectly pronounce the Indian word as "Chillicothe," calling it "Old Chillicothe," or later simply "Old Town." It was a Shawnee capital from 1774 to 1780. The Shawnee often used the name "Chillicothe" to describe important villages. Early pioneers designated one of the other Chillicothe towns, in Ross County, as Ohio's first capital.

Prehistoric Native American Sites

Fort Ancient near Lebanon and many other prehistoric Indian village sites and mounds that dot the region support that idea. SunWatch Indian Village, built by the Fort Ancient Indians 800 years ago, was discovered by amateur archeologists in the 1960s. The proposed expansion of a nearby sewage treatment plant in the 1970s prompted salvage excavation by the Dayton Society of Natural History, who preserved and reconstructed the Native American houses and poles on their original sites.

Many towns in this region still have their Indian names, such as Maumee, Piqua and Wapakoneta. Some other places that once were Indian now have English names, such as Bellefontaine (Blue Jacket's Town), Zanesfield (Tarhe the Crane's Town, before he gave it to Isaac Zane as a wedding present) and St. Johns (Black Hoof's Town). And some old Indian villages have only approximate modern locations, such as Buckongehelas' Town (northwest of Bellefontaine). But the Native American heritage here is unmistakable.

Fred A. Shaw, Shawnee descendant

SunWatch Indian Village/Archeological Park, a recreated Native American Village on the Great Miami River in Dayton (De Young)

Patterson Homestead , home of Col. Robert Patterson, founder of Lexington, Kentucky and co-founder of Cincinnati. (Woody)

Col. Patterson purchased Daniel Cooper's farm in 1803 and built his two-story brick home "Rubicon" there in 1816. Patterson's grandson, John Patterson, grew up at the Rubicon farm, and later built NCR on Cooper's old land. Col. Patterson also bought other land, giving him a total of 2117 acres which stretched east from Soldiers' Home (the VA) to Shakertown Pike, and included the land where a Catholic university is now located.

Land North of Ohio River Coveted

The land northwest of the Ohio River was coveted by many. To the Indians, it meant good fields for growing corn, beans and squash, and it meant hunting grounds for game. To the French, it meant abundance in natural resources, especially beaver and deer hides, valuable in the European market. To the English and American colonists, it meant the chance to start families, have their own land and establish their own farms, something that their European ancestors could never do.

The French and Indian War (1756-1763) ended the French claims to the territory, allowing the British to claim the abandoned French forts, and planted the seeds of the American Revolution.

British and Indian Allies

During the American Revolution (1775-1783) the British convinced the Indians living in the Northwest Territory (today's Ohio, Michigan, Indiana, Illinois and Wisconsin) that they would be better off if the American colonists never became free and independent, and that as allies the British and the Indians could prevent the further intrusion of settlers. At the same time, the British hoped the pioneer families would turn to them for protection, thus bringing the frontier under British control.

Pioneer Militias

The British plan backfired. The pioneers formed their own volunteer militias from Kentucky and fought both the British and the Indians. In addition, the British-Indian alliance caused a fear and hatred of Indians that would govern the relationship between settlers and Indians for many years to come.

On the frontier the violence was not confined to soldiers and battlefields, like the war in the eastern colonies. On the frontier, everything, and everybody, even women and children, were targets.

George Rogers Clark

Harsh times may engender extraordinary leaders, sometimes using brutal tactics. One such leader was George Rogers Clark. Over six feet tall with flaming red hair, the general was a commanding figure, and at 28 already famous for his cunning and success against the French in Vincennes, Illinois.

He knew how to get the most out of his men and he knew how to defeat Indians. As the only American general operating in the Northwest Territory, his tactics were simple: surprise, attack, destroy villages, torture prisoners, and burn crops to deflate the will to fight. Without homes and a steady food supply, the warring Indians and their families would starve.

Battle of Peckuwe

In 1780, in the first of two expeditions to the area, Clark organized about 1,000 volunteers and came up the Little Miami River from Cincinnati, to retaliate against recent Shawnee raids. On their way, they saw that the Shawnee village of Old Chillicothe (Old Town) had been burned and abandoned. In August a battle took place at the Shawnee village of Peckuwe (Old Piqua) on the Mad River, the site of today's George Rogers Clark Historic Park near Springfield. After a fight of several hours, the Indians fled. Clark's forces included Simon Kenton and Robert Patterson. Clark burned the Indian crops and cabins, forcing the 4,000-member Shawnee tribe to move to the Big Miami River, where they built a new town also called Piqua.

Clark's Second Expedition to the Area

In a second expedition in November 1782, Clark and his militia, including Daniel Boone, Simon Kenton, Robert Patterson and James Galloway, marched without hindrance until they reached the site of Dayton at the mouth of the Mad River. There they were met by Indians. A small skirmish ensued. The whites were victorious and spent the night before going on to Upper Piqua on the Great Miami River and destroying that Shawnee town. This was reportedly 14-year-old Tecumseh's first military encounter, and his only time to ever run from a battle. The success of Clark at the two Piqua towns and other places helped guarantee that the Northwest Territory would be part of the new United States.

Treaty of Fort Finney

Fort Finney (1785-1789) was the first permanent fort between the Great and Little Miami Rivers. Erected on the Ohio River at the mouth of the Great Miami, and west of Cincinnati's future site, it was in 1786 the site of a treaty with the Shawnee. The Indians gave up their land in Southwestern Ohio and Southern Indiana, and the whites agreed to keep white settlers off Indian land. Isaac Zane, George Rogers Clark, Tarhe the Crane and Buckongehelas were among those who signed it.

Galloway Cabin, Xenia, home of James Galloway, whose daughter Rebecca reportedly spent many hours nearby reading books with the Shawnee Tecumseh (Woody)

Tell me, Miami,
how it was with thee

When years ago Tecumseh
in his prime

His birch boat o'er thy
waters sent,

And pitched upon thy
banks his tent.

Paul Laurence Dunbar

Fort Recovery, built on site of St. Clair's defeat by order of General Wayne, to show pioneer resolve (J. Ostendorf)

Fort Washington, Cincinnati, where John Van Cleve, great-great-grandfather of Wilbur and Orville Wright, was scalped by Indians as he tended his garden in 1790 (unknown artist)

Cincinnati and Fort Washington

In 1788 John Cleves Symmes and Col. Robert Patterson founded Losantville (Cincinnati) on the Ohio River, opposite the mouth of Kentucky's Licking River. Neither the settlers nor the Indians kept to the terms of the Treaty of Fort Finney. In 1789 Fort Washington was built at Losantiville to help settlers defend themselves. In 1791 a young Virginian, William Henry Harrison, entered the army at the fort. While there he met Judge Symmes' daughter Anne, whom he married in 1795.

General Arthur St. Clair's Humiliating Defeat

After the Revolutionary War, the young nation turned westward to the area northwest of the Ohio River. This new Northwest Territory was America's future, and the Ohio Territory was key to exploring the rich grounds of Indiana, Michigan, Illinois and Wisconsin. President Washington was eager to clear the area of Indians so that the country could expand. He made General Arthur St. Clair, a Revolutionary War hero, Governor of the Territory, and ordered him to pacify the Indians. In September 1791 St. Clair set off from Fort Washington toward Kekionga, capital of the Miami Indians near today's Fort Wayne, Indiana. On the way he built Fort Hamilton (Hamilton) and Fort Jefferson (in Darke County). The Americans were not ready for the dawn attack November 4, 1791 which turned out to be the greatest single defeat in American military history. Each side had about the same number of forces, but St. Clair lost about 600 while the Miami, Shawnee, Delaware and others under Chief Little Turtle and Blue Jacket lost less than 100. The loss at the Battle of the Wabash represented one-third of the standing American army. The army fled in complete unorganized retreat, barely making it back to Fort Jefferson.

Fort Washington at Losantiville (Cincinnati) was "one of the most solid, substantial wood fortresses" on the western frontier. It served as a base of operations in the 1790s for expeditions of new settlers to Ohio and for military expeditions launched against the Native Americans in Ohio.

Dan Herle

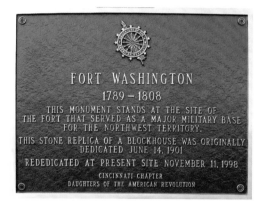

Fort Washington Plaque, marking original location of Fort Washington. Plaque is mounted on the side wall of the building at the corner of Fourth and Lawrence Streets, facing east, just west of the entrance of Lytle Park, Cincinnati, Ohio (E. Ostendorf)

It's easy to recall the early struggles of Dayton, when I see street signs such as Washington, St. Clair, Wabash, Kenton, Tecumseh, Wyandot, Delaware, Wayne, Patterson and Van Cleve.

Craig Southerington

Muncie, Indiana is named for the Munsee or Wolf tribe branch of the Delaware Indians who lived in Muncie c.1795-1836. After that, some went west, some stayed in Guernsey County, Ohio and some settled in Ashland and Richland Counties (Ohio). The Munsee Delaware or Wolf tribe has been identifiable as a tribe since 1000 A.D. and was in Pennsylvania, New Jersey, New York and Delaware.

Billy Little Soldier, Chief of the Munsee Delaware-USA Wolf Clan

Marker for birthplace of Tecumseh, Old Town (Brewer)

Fort Greenville encompassed a space the size of 50 football fields. The entire army of the U.S., over 3,000 men, Wayne's Legion, was garrisoned there. William Clark and Meriwether Lewis met there.

John Burkett

After nearly two centuries, the Indians of the Northeastern Woodlands and Great Lakes finally gave up the struggle to maintain their homeland against the press of encroaching whites. With the scratch of a pen at Greenville, they gave up most of Ohio and large portions of the Northwest Territory.

David Dixon

The loss of most of Ohio lands to native peoples by the Treaty of Greenville represents in our historical perspective the opening round of defeat in the ongoing war between the Native American Nations and the U.S. Federal Government. Despite the smoking of the sacred peace pipe and the burial of the hatchet, hundreds of treaties have been broken by the U.S. Government.

Raymond "Two Crows" Wallen
(Cherokee and Lumbie)

Shawnee Leader Tecumseh

Tecumseh, born reportedly near Old Chilllicothe (Old Town outside of Xenia), was 23 when he fought against St. Clair's army in 1791. Tecumseh later became a great leader, some say the greatest Indian leader ever in the United States. He was charismatic, well-liked and respected even by his enemies. He was gifted in languages and fought with both words and weapons to protect the rights of his people.

General Anthony Wayne Victorious at Fallen Timbers

The United States needed the right general. They found him in a fast-talking, whiskey-drinking, wild-eyed man: Anthony Wayne, known to many as Mad Anthony Wayne or just General Wayne. Crazy or not, in 1793 he and his army marched up north from Fort Washington, building forts along the way. In 1794 they defeated the Indians led by Blue Jacket and Little Turtle in the Battle of Fallen Timbers in present-day Maumee, close to Toledo. This was followed in 1795 by the Treaty of Greenville, signed by over 100 Indian representatives, at the enormous Fort Greenville built by Wayne two years earlier. Wayne and his aide William Henry Harrison were among the signers. This treaty opened to settlement most of Ohio, along with parts of Illinois, Indiana and Michigan.

Fort Wayne, Indiana: Kekionga

Built in 1794 by Gen. Wayne's soldiers, and located near where the St. Marys and the St. Joseph Rivers form the Maumee River, this newest fort's predecessors were at different times under French, British, Indian and American military control. Dating back to the 1670s, the site was originally called Kekionga and was the capital and largest of all the villages of the Miami Indians, and the home of the confederation with the Shawnee and others. It was from here that Little Turtle and Blue Jacket set out to attack settlers as far away as Pennsylvania. It was to Kekionga that three different generals (Harmar, St. Clair and Wayne) had been sent for the purpose of destroying it, before one finally succeeded in defeating the Indian Confederation in 1794. It was here that Chief Little Turtle was born and died.

Treaty of Greenville Marker, site of signing, West Main at Elm Street, Greenville (J. Ostendorf)

Tarhe the Crane (W)
(holding a peace pipe)

Little Turtle (M)

Buckongehelas (D)

Isaac Zane
(interpreter and white son-in-law
of Tarhe the Crane)

**Meriwether
Lewis**

William Clark
(younger brother of
George Rogers Clark)

Blue Jacket (S)

William Wells
(interpreter and white son-
in-law of Little Turtle)

**Anthony
Wayne**

**William
Henry
Harrison**

Indian Tribes: (D) = Delaware (M) = Miami (S) = Shawnee (W) = Wyandot

Treaty of Greenville Painting (Chandler/courtesy of the Ohio Historical Society)

When you arise in the morning, give thanks for the morning light, for your life and strength. Give thanks for your food and the joy of living. If you see no reason for giving thanks, the fault lies with yourself.

Tecumseh

Kenton's Gauntlet Marker, route 68N, near Old Town (Brewer)

First Settlers' Marker, under the pavillion at water's edge at Riverscape, on Monument and St. Clair St., marking where first settlers landed in 1796 (J.Ostendorf)

There are two sites connected to the Battle of Tippecanoe. One is the site of the village established in 1808 by The Prophet and Tecumseh, Prophetstown, run by Prophetstown State Park.

The other is the site of the battle, on a hill about a mile away at the Battlefield, under the auspices of the Tippecanoe County Historical Association.

Andy Pike

Tecumseh's War and the Battle of Tippecanoe

Tecumseh, who had fought at Fallen Timbers, refused to sign the Greenville Treaty. He and his brother The Prophet re-established Tippecanoe, an old Indian village at the Wabash and Tippecanoe Rivers near Lafayette, Indiana. Then Tecumseh recruited tribes to join a confederacy to drive the settlers away. By 1811 about 1,000 Indians had arrived at the new village of Prophetstown. While Tecumseh was away during one of his recruiting trips, William Henry Harrison camped nearby with over 1,000 men, providing an easy lure to The Prophet, who told the assembled tribes they could not be harmed. The Indians attacked at dawn on November 7, 1811 in the Battle of Tippecanoe, were defeated and fled. The confederacy collapsed. Tecumseh joined the British in the War of 1812 and was killed in 1813 at the Battle of the Thames in another conflict led by Harrison.

Simon Kenton

Also fighting in the Battle of the Thames was the frontiersman Simon Kenton, whose backwoods adventures laid the groundwork for settlement in both Kentucky and Ohio. He was a friend of Daniel Boone, accompanying him on many trips across Kentucky before exploring the new Northwest Territory. Kenton served under George Rogers Clark twice. He was captured and ran the gauntlet many times. Though Kenton was 15 years older than Tecumseh, their paths crossed frequently and it is said they held each other in mutual respect and fear. Tecumseh's death marked the end of Kenton's fighting days as well. Having come to Springfield around 1799, Kenton moved in 1815 to Zanesfield, where he died peacefully at 81 in 1836.

Settlers Rush in after Treaty of Greenville

After, and even before, the first Treaty of Greenville, pioneers rushed into the valley of the Miami River. Many cities were settled between 1796 and 1810, including Dayton, Centerville, Miamisburg, Springfield, Troy, Xenia, Piqua and Waynesville.

Daniel Cooper, Father of the City of Dayton

The city of Dayton was named after one of the investors who negotiated to buy land from the federal government, survey it, establish towns and resell land to settlers. The site was a prime location because of the rivers and fertile soil, and was ideal for mills and other early industry. Congressman Jonathan Dayton never saw his town. But Daniel Cooper, who came to survey the land for Mr. Dayton, laid out roads, donated land, started a sawmill, gristmill and other businesses and spent his whole life in Dayton.

In 1796 he built a cabin at the site of the Engineers' Club and lived there about two years. He acquired 1,000 acres south of town, where he built another cabin and created a hog farm. In 1803 he married Sophia Greene, sold his farm to Col. Robert Patterson, and moved to town, building a third cabin, this one where Talbott Tower is located.

Newcom Tavern, Dayton's oldest building (built 1796), now at Carillon Park (Perry)

First Daytonians Arrive

The first settlers to arrive in Dayton came by pirogue and poled up the Great Miami River. After an 11-day journey they arrived on April 1, 1796. Coming from Kentucky, they had traveled north up the river from Fort Washington. Their leader was Samuel Thompson. Among the 12 adults and children in the group were John Van Cleve's widow, Catherine Van Cleve Thompson (whom Samuel had married in 1792).

Dayton Platted

When they stepped onto the riverbank at today's Monument Avenue, the settlers found a tree with the name "St. Clair" scratched on it, to mark the first street south. Other streets were "Jefferson," "Main," "Ludlow"and "Wilkinson." "Dayton" was a simple paper map by surveyors Daniel Cooper and Israel Ludlow, and a few blazed trees. The settlers cleared trees and built cabins, many of them on Water Street (Monument), like Col.George Newcom's cabin, which served as schoolhouse, church, courthouse, jail, tavern and inn: on the southwest corner of Main and Water Streets.

In 1799 a blockhouse was built in the middle of Main and Water Streets for protection against Indians. It served instead as a schoolhouse for teacher Benjamin Van Cleve. A century later, when Central High School closed, the magnificent Steele High School with its cast-bronze lion mascot was erected nearby. Poet Paul Laurence Dunbar graduated from Central High School in 1891 in its last class, getting his diploma on stage in the Grand Opera House (Victoria Theatre).

Samuel Thompson was the leader of the first band of settlers in Dayton and was truly the first citizen of Dayton.

Lawrence Kent, Thompson's
4th great-grand-nephew

Daniel Cooper brought the first African American to his farm in 1802 as his servant. She later had two children who were indentured to him until adulthood.

Margaret Peters

Stately Steele High School, on the southeast corner of Main Street and Monument Avenue from 1894 to 1955, was named after educator Robert Steele, whose home is now the Dayton Women's Club. Steele High School graduated generations of students,including educator, author and journalist Roz Young. Katherine Wright, sister to Wilbur and Orville, taught Latin at Steele from 1898 to 1908.

Nancy Horlacher

Bob and I got married at Westminster in 1945. It was beautiful, with the Tiffany stained glass sanctuary windows, photos by Wallace Martin, and pastor Hugh Ivan Evans' words: "Never go to bed angry. Do things together."

Bebe Bates

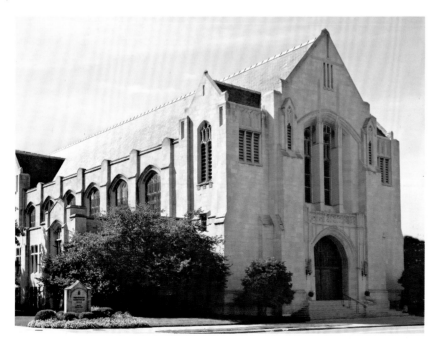

Westminster Presbyterian Church, on Wilkinson Street, home of Dayton's oldest congregation, dating from 1799 when it held services in a log cabin at the northeast corner of Third and Main. In 1818 Daniel Cooper died after moving a bell in a wheelbarrow for the congregation. (De Young)

In the grist mill business you literally have to "keep your nose to the grindstone" because if you don't stoop down to smell the two grindstones, you won't catch the signal that your grain is burning, probably because it is being fed too slowly!

Terry Clark

Without the canal, Dayton's settlement and economic growth would have been much slower, because the route by pirogue up the Great Miami River was difficult. By canal boat, though, the trip was calm and peaceful, for people and for goods.

Leon Bey

If you aren't watching for it, you might miss Canal Lock Park, at the intersection of Fishburg and Endicott in Huber Heights. The restored lock no. 70 and footpath is a good place to escape for some peace and quiet.

Celeste Boehm

In 1849, the Sisters of Notre Dame de Namur came by way of the Miami-Erie Canal from Cincinnati, to open their first permanent house founded outside of that city, at the corner of Ludlow and Franklin Streets in Dayton. They taught the girls at the Elementary School for Emmanuel Parish from 1849 to 1954. In 1886 they also opened a secondary school for girls on Ludlow, Notre Dame Academy, which continued until 1927 when it moved to Homewood Avenue, becoming Julienne High School, and remaining there until 1973.

Sister Louanna Orth, S.N.D. de N.

Area Grows

Settlers continued to arrive. Ohio became a state in 1803. Montgomery County was established in 1804. Dayton was the county seat, with Newcom's Tavern the temporary seat of justice.

Mills

Since the time of Daniel Cooper, who built the first mills in the region, mills have been an integral part of the Miami Valley. Sawmill and Stonemill Roads near the Patterson Homestead remind us of this early industry. In the 1860s there were more than 1,200 water-powered grist mills in Ohio. Only a few remain. Peerless Mill Inn in Miamisburg marks the site of a gristmill and sawmill powered by the waters of the Miami-Erie Canal in 1828. Only the sawmill exists today, converted in 1929 into a restaurant.

Miami-Erie Canal

The coming of the Miami and Erie Canal made the bounty of the Miami Valley available to the world. The canal went from the Ohio River near Cincinnati to Toledo and included most of the

Clifton Mill, on the Little Miami River (Brewer)

cities in between: Hamilton, Middletown, Franklin, Miamisburg, West Carrollton, Dayton, Tippecanoe (Tipp City), Troy, Piqua, Sidney, Minster, New Bremen, St. Marys and Defiance. Started in 1825 and completed in 1845, it was an important means of transportation for about 30 years.

William Henry Harrison's Town

One of the canal towns which seemed to spring up overnight was Tipp City, named after William Henry Harrison, who had been called "Old Tippecanoe" after the Battle of Tippecanoe. A political rally in Dayton, by then a city of some 6,000, drew a huge crowd and reportedly started his famous "log cabin" presidential campaign for the election of 1840. Harrison gave "stump" speeches in Chillicothe, Columbus and elsewhere, and was perhaps the first to develop a modern political campaign, with songs, party insignia, meeting and slogans like "Tippecanoe and Tyler too." Harrison became President but died after 30 days in office.

Other Canal Towns

Other towns benefited from the canal. A farmer or manufacturer in Eton, Troy, Tipp City or Germantown, for example, could now sell goods in Cincinnati, Louisville or even New Orleans. In turn, the canal opened the Miami Valley to world markets. One area manufacturer, G. Stomps & Company (later "Stomps-Burkhardt"), was located on the canal and used it to ship wooden chairs during most of the company's history (1859-1928). In Dayton the canal bed was filled in and became Patterson Blvd., a major road through the city. The Armory building and buildings housing Canal Street Tavern, Southern Belle, and Hauer Music date from that era. The same can be said of Middletown, where Verity Parkway (Route 4) follows the old canal route. In Piqua some of the buildings on Main Street seem to have two fronts because the rear of the buildings once faced the canal. Minster and other towns still have their sections of the canal fully intact.

Canal Brings Settlers from Abroad

The canal also brought more people: German, Irish, Hungarian, Polish, Lithuanian and others. In some places it became common to hear German spoken as much as English. In Dayton some church services were held in German and some newspapers were printed in German as late as the 1920s and 1930s. An immigrant from Germany could get on a boat, cross the ocean, get on a canal boat in New York harbor and take it to the Great Lakes, board another boat to Toledo and ride a second canal boat all the way to Dayton, before his feet touched dry land.

A Stomps-Burkhardt Roman or Bishop's Chair (Cercone)

In 1992 Bill Turner showed me around a building he owned on Patterson Boulevard (the current Miami-Jacobs Career College Building). He pointed out a dirty water mark about eight feet from the floor, and said that the 1913 flood caused the canal to overflow to that level.

Antonette Flohre

When I was a boy in the 1940s, everybody in the Minster-New Bremen area spoke German. I could hardly speak English.

Merinus Puthoff

My father left Italy in 1920. In 1954 he went back to Giuliano di Roma, his hometown. When he returned to Dayton, he told my mother: "Not a stone has turned since I left Giuliano, but in America I learned English, got a job, married and had children, opened a successful restaurant and created a whole new life for myself." I feel sure that his experience is common to immigrants from all around the world.

Gloria Anticoli

Madonna of the Trail, National Road , Old Rt. 40 West, west of Springfield, honoring pioneer mothers traveling by covered wagon (De Young)

Vandalia, Illinois was the intended destination of the Old National Road. When it looked as if construction might not reach there, settlers here in Ohio named their town Vandalia.

Arlene Setzer

At its peak in the mid-1800s, the Watervliet Shaker community had about 100 members. The Lebanon Shakers had about 200.

Joyce Grabill

Katherine McColloch reportedly joined the Lebanon Shakers after three husbands were killed by Indians. About 1780 she married Silas Zane, oldest of six siblings: Ebenezer, Jonathan, Andrew, Isaac and Betty, who were the first settlers of Wheeling, Zanesfield and Zanesville.

[editor]

National Road

The area experienced phenomenal economic growth with the coming of the National Road. The National Road was the country's first national highway—the first road created for travel by Conestoga wagon or other vehicle rather than on foot. Authorized in 1806 by Congress, the road extended west 700 miles across five states from Cumberland, Maryland to Illinois, using the new "macadam" surface—several layers of compacted broken stone. It reached Springfield, Ohio in 1838 and Vandalia, Illinois in 1840.

It was successful in opening up Ohio and much of the Old Northwest Territory to settlement, creating new towns, stimulating growth in others and providing access to eastern markets. The added capital meant new industries and a quickly changing streetscape in most of our cities.

Dayton's Old Courthouse

One new structure was the Montgomery County Courthouse in the center of Dayton, built on land donated by Daniel Cooper. Started in 1847 and completed in 1850, this imposing structure boasted a stone roof, running water and an elliptical courtroom. It is considered one of the finest examples of Greek Revival architecture in America and was the site of a political speech by soon-to-be President Abraham Lincoln, campaigning in the fall of 1859.

Miami Valley Shakers

The 1850s were also the peak time for a communitarian group popularly called "Shakers" because of their enthusiasm during church services. An offshoot of the Quakers, they believed in a simple, pacifist, celibate, self-sustaining and communitarian life which was agrarian-based. They marketed seeds on a wide scale for sale to outsiders and are known for their simple, practical furniture and elegant boxes.

The first and largest Shaker community west of the Alleghenies was Union Village, established in 1805, four miles west of Lebanon, Ohio. Between 1805-1920 almost 1,000 Shakers lived at the 4,500-acre-site, where the Otterbein Home is now located.

The second Shaker community in the area was the Watervliet community, founded on land now occupied by the Miami Valley Research Park and Bergamo. Two buildings from the Watervliet community are now at the Kettering-Moraine Museum.

Lebanon's Golden Lamb, Ohio's oldest inn, where many Shaker paintings and artifacts are displayed (Woody)

Cemetery at Veterans' Administration Medical Center, the nation's third oldest Soldiers' Home, created for Civil War veterans by one of the last pieces of legislation signed by President Lincoln before his assassination in April 1865 (Woody)

Private Fair Monument, in honor of Civil War veterans, near Monument Ave. and Main Street, looking north across Main Street Bridge. On southwest corner: Newcom Manor (Insco Bldg.), original site of Newcom Tavern. On southeast corner (not visible): CareSource Bldg., former site of Steele High School (Makley)

National Afro-American Museum, located on the old campus of Wilberforce University (De Young)

Railroads

Railroads soon became more popular than canals. The Little Miami Railroad was an important early Ohio railroad built from 1837-1848 and connecting Cincinnati to Springfield. It is now a bike path. The Dayton and Union Railroad came through Trotwood in 1852 and is commemorated by the restored Trotwood Depot Museum in Olde Town.

The Civil War

The Civil War (1861-1865) was a time of great tribulation. Ohio gave more troops to the Union cause than any other northern state, and Greene County gave more troops per capita than any other county, yet the area was divided. Many families had strong southern state ties or did not think that freeing slaves was worth so much northern blood. Many others felt strongly about the preservation of the Union.

The Underground Railway

For years local abolitionists had silently, passionately, and at great risk to themselves, been carrying on a secret war on slavery by becoming conductors and keepers of safe houses along the famous Underground Railroad. Blacks seeking to flee bondage found guidance, comfort and hope from a hidden network of heroes in places like Springfield, Dayton, and Wilberforce University, founded in 1856, named for English abolitionist William Wilberforce, and now the oldest private African-American University in the U.S.

Copperheads form Anti-War/Anti-Lincoln Movement

Dayton was also the headquarters for the anti-war, anti-Lincoln group known as the Copperheads. Clement Vallandigham, a lawyer, newspaper publisher and congressman from Dayton, led a group of Democrats opposed to the Civil War. They called themselves "Sons of Liberty." Most people referred to them as Copperheads partly because of their chosen symbol, a pin made from the image of an Indian head cut from a copper penny, and partly because most supporters of the war considered them traitors or poisonous "snakes in the grass."

President Lincoln and the Soldiers' Home

The lasting symbol of the Civil War locally was the creation of the Old Soldiers' Home (today's Veterans' Administration Medical Center) in Dayton. The veterans' facility at West Third St. and Gettysburg Ave. boasted a hospital, a national cemetery, a garden, a zoo with exotic animals, and a cyclorama of the Battle of Gettysburg. The Soldiers' Home in Dayton was also the home of Paul Laurence Dunbar's father, who had brought his family here to get the medical services offered to him as a veteran of the Union cause.

When asked to make caissons to carry Civil War cannon, the Studebaker Wagon Company, run by two Studebakers/ members of the Church of the Brethren, split in half. One brother was opposed to profiting from the war. The other was attracted by the opportunity: his company eventually made Studebaker automobiles.

Kenneth Irwin

Clement Vallandigham ran for Ohio governor in 1863, denouncing the Lincoln administration and declaring the effort to subdue the South a failure. If Vallandigham won, said Republicans, he might call on other governors in the Old Northwest to form a new nation that would cut the East adrift and give the South independence.

Carl Becker

Paul Laurence Dunbar Home (Woody)

The Annie I know was a diminutive Victorian lady who became a role model for 20th-century women. She grew up in abject poverty but that did not deter her from becoming successful. Not only competing but also triumphing in an area that had previously been dominated by men, she firmly believed that women should learn to shoot so that they could take care of themselves. Annie became an international superstar, but she never forgot her family and her roots in Darke County.

Penny Perry

We switched from a suburban church to an inner-city church, St. Benedict the Moor's, and found it as welcoming and loving as our families back home on the coasts.

Paula and David Block

The Centerville Ministerial Association has been a source of Christian support for ministers from 30 churches of different denominations.

Pastor Winston Baldwin

Annie Oakley

Born just before the Civil War, Annie Mosey started hunting at age nine in order to take care of her widowed mother and her siblings. She never went to school but paid off her mother's mortgage, advancing the cause of women in general, and show-business women in particular, by being the little five-foot-tall sharpshooter from Greenville. Changing her name to Oakley, she made her first public performance in Springfield in 1880.

Called Little Sure Shot by Indian Chief Sitting Bull, Annie could outshoot any man alive and was a star in Buffalo Bill's Wild West Show. Annie and her husband Frank Butler joined the famous show in 1885. They had met in Cincinnati, when a traveling vaudevillian with a sharp-shooting act challenged all comers to a contest of marksmanship. Annie beat Frank and he fell in love with her on the spot.

Statue of Annie Oakley, Annie Oakley Memorial Park, Greenville (Wyckoff)

Early Churches and Synagogues

By 1888, residents of Dayton had the choice of 46 places of worship, including 38 Protestant churches, seven Catholic churches and one Jewish synagogue. At about the same time Springfield also had a synagogue as well as 40 churches.

Early Colleges and Universities

Many colleges and universities were founded in the area in the nineteenth century. The oldest public college is Miami University, founded in 1809. Wittenberg University was founded by the Lutheran Synod of Ohio in 1845. Defiance College, affiliated with the United Church of Christ, was started in 1850. That same year the Society of Mary, a Catholic Order, founded St. Mary's Institute on a farm south of Dayton. Antioch College was founded in 1852 by the Christian Church. Miami Jacobs Career College opened in 1860, and Cedarville College (currently with a Baptist affiliation) was started in 1887.

Pulley Carillon Bell Tower, Miami University, founded 1809, second oldest public college west of the Alleghenies, alma mater of John H. Patterson and home of the McGuffey Readers. Daniel Cooper was made trustee in 1815. (De Young)

Piqua is a great community to raise my children and give them the opportunity to obtain a Catholic education.

Linda Peltier

Ever since the first settlers in Dayton, the Jewish community has made a significant contribution to the business, educational, medical, and professional life of the region.

Stanley Blum

We are indeed fortunate to have many school choices in the Miami Valley. We are equally fortunate to have many area schools that consistently demonstrate outstanding learning achievement by their students.

Donald E. Overly

I remember when my cousins, the Horvaths, lived in the other side of our Salem Ave. duplex across from the Jewish Temple. Allan's and my bedrooms were separated by a thin interior wall, ideal for Morse Code communication.

Below our bedroom windows, a single tin roof covered the kitchen extensions. When we were eight years old, when the lights were out, one of us would climb onto this roof and climb in the other's bedroom. But then our mothers discovered us, denied us dessert and nailed the windows shut!

Allan and I managed to grow up safe and sound – he, a geologist and photographer, and I, a heart surgeon.

Jerry Grismer

Health care in the Miami Valley is the largest single employer, larger even than WPAFB.

Daniel Schoulties

I met Esther Price Candies when I moved here in 1966 and love them to this day.

Dinah Garrison

Cassano's is the best and cheesiest pizza in the area!

Sherlean McCombs

Dorothy Lane Market began as a fruit stand opened by Calvin Mayne and his partner Frank Sakada on the corner of Dorothy Lane and Far Hills Avenue in 1948. Ownership has been in the Mayne family for three generations and there now are three stores.

Norman Mayne

Pre-Civil War Companies

The, Mead Corporation, a Dayton company that would eventually become Meadwestvaco, was started in 1846 by Col. Daniel Mead and his partners as a paper manufacturer.

The Barney and Smith Car Company started to make elegant wooden railroad cars in Dayton in 1849, a time when there were no railroads in town. The owners foresaw a coming need. Ironically, they had to transport the cars by canal boat to the Ohio River, where they were shipped on the nearest railroad to their destination.

Early Hospitals

Soldiers' Home had a hospital but the first public hospital was St. Elizabeth's, which opened in 1878, followed by Springfield's Community Hospital in 1887 and Dayton's Protestant Deaconess (Miami Valley) Hospital in 1890.

The Arcade and Food Vendors

Built in 1902, the Arcade was one of the most popular places to shop for unusual fruit and vegetables, meat and seafood, baked goods and fresh-cut flowers. A complex of five connected buildings topped by a glass-domed rotunda, it was an early "shopping mall."

Interior arches leading to the great dome of Arcade (Murphy)

Third Street entrance to historic Arcade (Woody)

Vendor Daniel W. Mikesell, whose company is now the oldest potato chip company in the U.S., started selling his foodstuffs in horse-drawn or motor vehicles soon afterward.

Post-Civil War Companies

After the Civil War, the Miami Valley was there to meet the needs of a growing nation.

In 1866, Lucius Reynolds and his brother-in-law founded a business forms company in Downtown Dayton, later called Reynolds and Reynolds, and specializing in automotive dealer software and services.

In 1875, John T. Hartzell opened a sawmill in Greenville. The company moved to Piqua, and the family to Oakwood. In 1914 new neighbor Orville Wright encouraged young Robert to build aircraft propellers. He did, and the firm later was called Hartzell Propeller.

By 1880 William Whiteley's Champion Company produced more farm machinery than all the factories in Chicago put together. Sold to International Harvester, it peaked in Springfield in 1979.

In 1884 John H. Patterson formed a new Dayton company, the National Cash Register (NCR), to sell a product nobody seemed to want but soon could not live without, the cash register.

George P. Huffman's newly purchased Davis Sewing Machine Company took a gamble in 1894 and began manufacturing bicycles, responding to a craze that was sweeping the nation.

In 1897, the Hobart Manufacturing Company was founded in Troy and introduced mechanization in food production.

In 1900 George Verity opened a plant in Middletown. The next year he renamed his company American Rolling Mill Company (ARMCO), later called AK Steel, a major employer there for over 100 years..

Wright Bicycles

Two brothers in Dayton, Wilbur and Orville Wright, caught hold of the bicycle craze and started a bicycle repair business. They moved their shop six times.

In 1896 they decided to introduce a line of their own handmade bicycles with their St. Clair and Van Cleve models. When the market for handmade bicycles was slow, the brothers focused their talents elsewhere.

Horace Greeley may be known for the quote "Go West, young man," but it was Springfield, Ohio that made it possible for a young man to tame the prairie. From the Civil War to WWII, Springfield reigned supreme in the booming farm machinery business.

Michael E. Haubner

My father, Arthur Kramer, used to get his bicycle repaired at the Wright Brothers' shop on Third near Broadway. He lived for awhile at 20 S. Hawthorn across from the Wrights at number 7. One day Katharine Wright asked him to tell the neighbors that if they piled their leaves in front of the house, she would pay for a truck to take the leaves away.

Sister Marjorie Kramer, S.N.D. de N.

Wright Cycle Co., Wright Brothers' bicycle shop at its original location at 22 S. Williams Street. (Woody)

I used to deliver Bordens milk at the side door of Hawthorn Hill. Sometimes I'd see Orville Wright on Harman Ave. and say: "Hello, Mr. Wright" and he'd respond: "Good morning".

Ray G. Wertz

In 1948 I was 9 years old. My grandmother and I took the bus one day from East Dayton to watch Orville Wright's funeral procession move through Downtown Dayton on its way to Woodland Cemetery.

Carl Evans

Wright-Patterson Air Force Base was at the center of considerable military history and played a critical role in early manned flight. Today thousands of military personnel, government civilians, and local citizens work hard to keep us all safe.

Dave Wooten

Aeroplanes

In 1903 Wilbur and Orville gave the world the "aeroplane." Working in their spare time, the brothers first studied the problems of flight and discovered that many earlier inventors had missed some fundamental facts about the science of flight. Testing their theories on their home-made wind tunnel, and methodically recording their data, the brothers soon had a working model of a flying machine.

With the help of local businesses like Requarth Lumber, which supplied the wood for the plane, and Buckeye Iron Works, which cast the aluminum engine block for the engine, the brothers were able to fly. They then worked on technical difficulties. Soon they had mastered all the elements of control, making modern airplanes possible.

White Scarves, Goggles and Leather Helmets

The brothers tested their machine in such places as McCook and Huffman Prairie Flying Fields, which later became part of Wright-Patterson Air Force Base.

Flying was dangerous but exciting. This was the era when some pilots wore white scarves, goggles and leather helmets. Weaver Aircraft Company (WACO) of Troy responded to the interest in civilian flying and built a variety of popular biplanes between 1919 and 1946, some still in use today.

Dayton's Flyover sculpture, reflecting the path of the Wright Brothers' first flight, looking north on Main street toward the Private Fair Monument (Murphy)

Dayton Air Show (Wyckoff)

Neil Armstrong Air & Space Museum, Wapakoneta (Brewer)

Hawthorn Hill, corner of Harman and Park Avenues in Oakwood. Built for the Wright Brothers, it was named for the street where they grew up in West Dayton (De Young)

Moraine Farm, 1233 W. Stroop Road, last home of Col. Edward Deeds. Orville Wright, a friend of Deeds, spent hours tinkering with mechanical things at his friend's home or resetting pins in the basement bowling alley for any bowler who happened to be visiting. (Woody)

First presidential plane, known as the Sacred Cow, built for President Franklin Delano Roosevelt. Now at U.S. Museum of the Air Force (Murphy)

Deeds Barn, where Kettering, Deeds et al invented self-starter; originally at 319 Central Ave., now at Kettering Moraine Museum (De Young)

Ridgeleigh Terrace, Kettering, built in 1914, home of inventor Charles Kettering. After burning down, it was rebuilt by his daughter-in-law Virginia Kettering and donated to Kettering Health Network. (Woody)

Kettering and Deeds

Creativity and invention seem to run at the very core of the Greater Dayton Region. It gave the world not only the airplane, but also inventions as simple as the mail chute, the stepladder and the pop-top opener by Dayton Reliable Tool's founder Ermal Fraze.

One of the area's native sons, Charles F. Kettering, brought to Dayton by NCR, is considered one of America's greatest inventors. With Col. Edward A. Deeds and Harold E. Talbott, he founded Dayton Engineering Laboratories Company ((Delco, later Delphi). Kettering had hundreds of patents, including the first electric automobile self-starter.

Kettering and Deeds also founded the Engineers' Club of Dayton to provide a meeting place for the area's many highly skilled engineers and technicians. In 1918 they erected the current building on E. Monument Ave.

The Self-starter

The self-starter solved the difficult problem of hand-cranking a car to start it. First used in the 1912 Cadillac, the self-starter greatly increased the market for automobiles. After World War I, the number of new auto dealerships grew significantly again. By 1927 Downtown Dayton dealers were selling Fords, Packards, Buicks, Chryslers and Chevrolets.

The world's first self-starters were manufactured for one year starting in 1911 on the fourth floor of the Beaver Power Building on Fourth Street and St. Clair, the new home of the St. Clair Lofts in Downtown Dayton. They made 8,000 of them. This was the beginning of DELCO.

Leon Bey

I still dream about the elevator at Stomps Chevrolet, where I worked. My uncle, Hank Grismer, service department head, sent me to Moline, Illinois to learn front-end alignment. I was 18 and got to visit my brother Euie who was studying art in Chicago.

Carroll Horvath

Red Packard Roadster, at America's Packard Museum, the only Packard Museum located in a restored dealership, with over 50 cars (Woody)

Dayton and World War II

In the early part of World War II, the British deciphered the German submarine codes. Then the Germans codes were refined and the British could no longer read them. By 1942 German U-boats sank 1,660 ships in the Atlantic.

While at NCR, Col. Deeds was approached for a top-secret project. The Navy wanted Joseph R. Desch, a brilliant young engineer, to design machines to crack German submarine codes. The Navy commandeered Building 26, NCR's old night school, an Art Deco structure at South Patterson and Stewart Streets. It created a naval base there: the U.S. Naval Computing Machine Laboratory. From 1942-1945, nearly 1,000 NCR and Navy personnel, including 600 Navy WAVES, worked on the computer-like machines. Desch's machines hastened the end of WWII by two years and saved thousands of lives!

Jim DeBrosse

I think it just to say that thousands of families – in the United States, Europe and Asia – exist today because battles were prevented or ended due to machines that left Building 26.

My father died before being able to tell me why he had received the Medal for Merit from President Truman, because the project was not declassified until 1992.

Debbie Desch Anderson

In actual physical output, Dayton probably contributed more to the war effort during World War II than other city. Activities at NCR, the GM and Delco plants, and WPAFB all point to Dayton as being essential to U.S. war efforts.

Jerry Hauer

U.S. Naval Computing Laboratory/ Building 26, NCR's old Night School, 1938 (courtesy The NCR Archive at Dayton History)

Personnel at Building 26, Joseph Desch, front row far left (courtesy The NCR Archive at Dayton History)

Sports

In the world of sports, the Miami Valley's presence is undeniable. The first game ever played between two teams that would become the National Football League (NFL) was played in Triangle Park in Dayton in 1920, and won by the Dayton Triangles. Coached by Nelson "Bud" Talbott, son of Harold E. Talbott, Sr., they were called the Dayton Triangles and sponsored by three factories founded by Edward Deeds and Charles Kettering. That same year an African-American baseball team, the Dayton Marcos, was one of eight teams in the newly-formed Negro League to play a full season. Hamilton's Joe Nuxhall, former pitcher and 35-year radio voice of the Cincinnati Reds, is remembered for his charm, wit and generosity. Olympians like David Albritton (1936), Edwin Moses (1976) and Kristin King call this area home, as does Baseball Hall of Fame's Mike Schmidt (1995).

Homer Bailey, now with the Cincinnati Reds, while pitching for the Dayton Dragons (photo courtesy of Dayton Dragons)

In fifth grade, my friends (usually Hugh O'Keefe, Jerry Dahm and Bob Musselman) and I would go to Triangle Park to play baseball so early that the morning dew was still on the grass and the ball got too wet to use. Then we'd skip stones on the Stillwater River.

Larry Horvath

The Dayton Dragons, our hometown team, bring fans and families together to enjoy what has to be the quintessential American experience: baseball on a warm summer evening!

Karen Schnee

Sculpture of the Wright Brothers and their plane, at main gate, Area B, WPAFB with Air Force Museum in background. The U.S. Museum of the Air Force is the oldest and largest military aviation museum in the world. (Murphy)

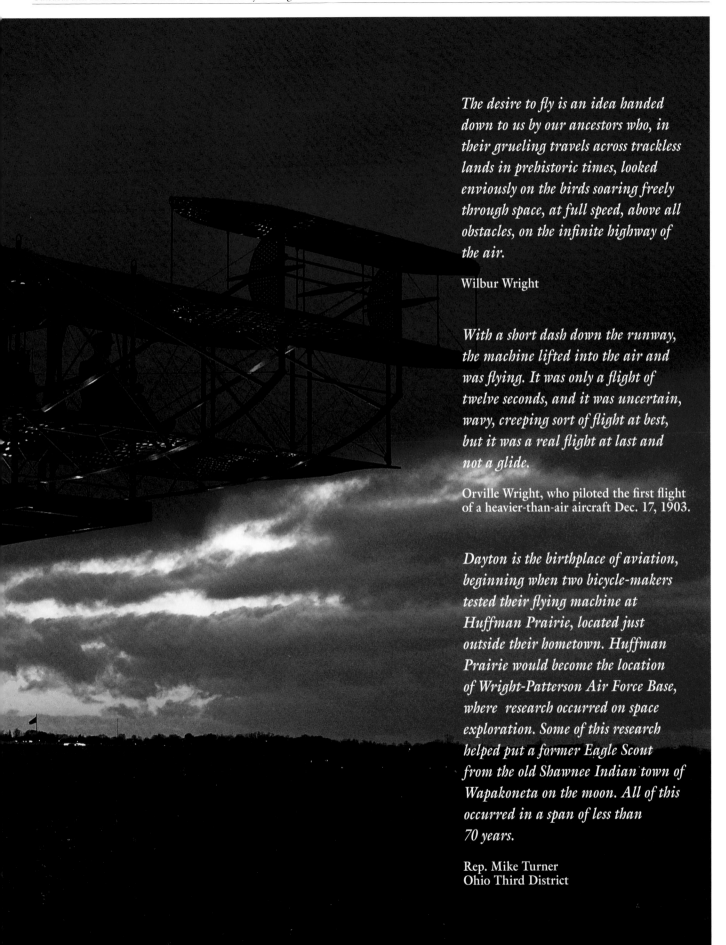

The desire to fly is an idea handed down to us by our ancestors who, in their grueling travels across trackless lands in prehistoric times, looked enviously on the birds soaring freely through space, at full speed, above all obstacles, on the infinite highway of the air.

Wilbur Wright

With a short dash down the runway, the machine lifted into the air and was flying. It was only a flight of twelve seconds, and it was uncertain, wavy, creeping sort of flight at best, but it was a real flight at last and not a glide.

Orville Wright, who piloted the first flight of a heavier-than-air aircraft Dec. 17, 1903.

Dayton is the birthplace of aviation, beginning when two bicycle-makers tested their flying machine at Huffman Prairie, located just outside their hometown. Huffman Prairie would become the location of Wright-Patterson Air Force Base, where research occurred on space exploration. Some of this research helped put a former Eagle Scout from the old Shawnee Indian town of Wapakoneta on the moon. All of this occurred in a span of less than 70 years.

Rep. Mike Turner
Ohio Third District

Culture Works provides grants and services to support the Miami Valley's rich and diverse cultural assets.

Nathan Smallwood

It is incredible how the Dayton Philharmonic Orchestra, the oldest and largest performing arts organization in the community, continues to innovate and thrive.

Judy McCormick

Springfield has a long history of arts and culture: with the Symphony, the Summer Arts Festival, StageWorks, Civic Theatre, Westcott House, the Museum of Art and other organizations.

Larry Coressel

Greater Dayton is theater rich! A buffet of high-quality venues produces more than 100 plays annually, thanks to many volunteer actors, directors and stage crews!

Burt Saidel

In the 1920s and 1930s Katherine Talbott promoted the choir of Dayton's Westminster Presbyterian Church in the U.S. and abroad. The choir became the Westminster Choir College in New Jersey. In Dayton today, the congregation's choir still strives for excellence.

John Neely

The Arts

Creativity does not stop with the invention of things. The arts have a long history here as well. Famous actors wuch as Sarah Bernhardt, Edwin Booth and Lily Langtry performed at the Victoria Theatre or its predecessors, the Turner Opera House, the Music Hall and the Grand Opera House. Uncle Tom's Cabin and Buffalo Bill Cody also came to town. Paul Laurence Dunbar's mother Matilda was among the subjects of world-famous Dayton photographer Jane Reece. Josephine and Hermene Schwarz, two sisters, founded the Dayton Ballet in 1937, the second oldest ballet company in America.

The region has long had world-class orchestras, choirs, art museums and performing arts centers, including the Dayton Philharmonic Orchestra, the Dayton Art Institute and the Victoria Theatre. Paul Katz started the Dayton Philharmonic in 1933; his brother Maurice wrote the program notes for it. Kettering's Fraze Pavillion, an outdoor amphitheatre, has drawn crowds since it began in 1991. Then in 2003, a new era for the region's arts began with the opening of the grand Benjamin and Marian Schuster Performing Arts Center in Downtown Dayton.

Dayton Ballet Company Studio, Victoria Theatre (Woody)

Dayton Art Institute, donated to the community by Julia Shaw Patterson Carnell (De Young)

The Dayton Art Institute is that cultural beacon on the hill that has served as the primary local venue for reflecting the artistic history of mankind from antiquity to the present.

Willis "Bing" Davis

Historic Victoria Theatre, one of many beneficiaries of philanthropist Virginia Kettering (De Young)

I like to think of the Dayton Art Institute as "Dayton's living room" where Daytonians of all backgrounds, ages and artistic tastes come together to celebrate art, each other and the community.

Brad Tillson

The Victoria Theatre. For many years my family has enjoyed the Dayton Ballet, the Dayton Philharmonic's Chamber Series and the Muse Machine which this great "lady" has hosted.

Ann Salyers

WDPR/WDPG, 24-hour classical music, Charles Wendelken-Wilson on the air (De Young)

I'm eternally proud to have been a part of the DPO's evolving musical fabric. From 1975 to 1987 the orchestra and I developed and matured together. Today it has blossomed into the Dayton Philharmonic of the 21st century, truly worthy of the great hall it now calls home.

Charles Wendelken-Wilson

Courts and hospitals are experiencing a growing need for interpreters not only of Spanish but also of Russian, Arabic and Hindi.

Tina Gonzalez

Commissioned by industrialist Burton Westcott and built in 1908, this home is quite impressive, even in the 21st century, as a home of exceptional space, light and functionality.

Sandra Bell

Women's Rights

What Annie Oakley championed in the late 19th century was taken up by many other women in the Women's Suffrage movement, providing for the right of women to vote and serve in political office. Dayton was a particularly strong center of this movement in Ohio. In 1869 women formed an early group at the Montgomery County Courthouse. Groups met to promote their cause at the Dayton YMCA, the Victoria Theatre and in the Schwind Building.

Multi-cultural Bounty

Dayton's Chaminade-Julienne High School, formed by the merger of Chaminade (for boys) and Julienne (for girls) at the original location of Notre Dame Academy, aptly reflects the multicultural character of the Greater Dayton Region. "C.J." attracts both Catholic and non-Catholic students from over 45 elementary schools.

John Patterson's Words Ring True

Much more could be said about the many institutions, individuals, events and places that make the Greater Dayton Region a unique and wonderful place to live. Their discovery is an unending adventure. Few places in America can boast the rich heritage we have here.

John H. Patterson once said, "We are part of all we have met." In the Miami Valley we meet a wealth of natural, historical and cultural treasures every day. These riches surround us, give us a sense of place and help make us who we are.

Westcott House, Springfield, first house designed by Frank Lloyd Wright after his trip to Japan (Brewer)

Dorothy Patterson was the daughter of John Patterson of NCR. Like her father, she loved to go horseback-riding on their property. Dorothy Lane was as far as she was allowed to go riding. Originally it was called "Dorothy's Lane."

Curt Dalton

Patterson Memorial, John H. Patterson on his favorite horse Spinner, Hills and Dales MetroPark (Haverstick)

Afterword

Did we make our lives so comfortable and withdrawn from reality that we cannot see the social sins that our silence is supporting? Only a profound change in our way of living – our values and attitudes – can bring new life to our world.

Dorothy Stang, S.N.D. de N.,
class of '49, Julienne High School

Perhaps the most fundamental lesson of peacemaking is derived from the old Hebrew adage: "Choose your enemy well, for he is what you will become."

However, the realization of this simple truth is a life-long pilgrimage to unite the will of the spirit to the work of the flesh, with this special observance: we are not required to be successful; we are only required to be faithful. Such a committed pilgrim is clearly made worthy of the long-promised blessing reserved for the peacemakers!

Martin Sheen (Ramon Estevez),
class of '58, Chaminade High School

As we rejoice in the unique richness of our Miami Valley, we ask ourselves what legacy we wish to leave future generations.

We believe that Dayton is known worldwide as a place that created peace where there was war. In Sarajevo a young woman said to us once, "Dayton is a sacred place because it stopped the killing."

So it seems that more than anything else, our Miami Valley home and our earth home need to leave a legacy of peace.

Peace that starts in our hearts and moves out to all other creatures.

Peace that is awed by the diversity in people, in animals and in plant life.

Peace that emphasizes healing our environment, and protecting and sharing the earth's natural resources of air, water and green space.

Peace that rejects violence and honors all other hearts with respect and understanding.

Peace that forgives others and ourselves, treating others as we would like to be treated.

Peace that knows that in the long run, what is good for others is also good for us.

Like the beautiful waters that come together in the Miami River, may this peace ripple ever onward, and fill our Miami Valley home and our earth home with its energy. In the words of an old campfire song, "Peace, we ask of thee, o river. Peace, peace, peace." *

Ralph and Christine Dull

* Song "Peace O River"
Words by Glendora Bosling, music by
Viola Wood, both from Greenville, Ohio

Dayton International Peace Museum (one of only two peace museums in the U.S.), in the historic Pollack House, former home of Botts Dancing School, moved from W. Third Street to Monument Avenue in 1977 (Brewer)

Index

LEGEND: MP–MetroPark   SP–State Park   HP–Historic Park

Quote Index

Glossary

Frontier Term	Meaning
Auglaize	fallen timbers
Chillicothe	principal fire
Erie	cat
Illinois	tribe of superior men
Indiana	land of Indians
Kekionga	blackberry patch
Kentucky	land of tomorrow
Losantiville	city across from the mouth of the Licking
Michigan	great lake
Ohio	great river
Tippecanoe	buffalo fish
Wapakoneta	clay river